Woman Up

*With love,
Nell ♡*

by
Nell Grecian

© "Copyright" Nell Grecian 2020

The author has asserted her moral rights.
No part of this book may be produced or transmitted in any form or by any means mechanical or electrical, including photocopying, without permission in writing, except by a reviewer in connection with a newspaper, magazine or broadcast.

ISBN: 978-1-913369-05-7
Blackhall Publishing

Cover photograph by Patch Dolan

Cover design by Abi Everett

Typesetting by Printspot (01289) 309217

Printed by Martins the Printers
Spittal, Berwick-upon-Tweed (01289) 306006

Nell Grecian currently lives in Oxfordshire with her boyfriend and crippling council tax. She spends her days working, writing and lying on the sofa, masturbating. Although she can't currently afford cereal, she has great hopes for the future and wishes to retire to Edinburgh as soon as possible, where she can watch her many, many children grow up, while she eats as many haggis suppers as she likes.

This is for anyone who needs a little reminder that having, talking about, writing about and enjoying sex is completely fucking normal and should be encouraged rather than shamed. Oh, and anyone who needs a laugh at my cringe-worthy stories to make themselves feel that bit better.

Above all; this is for the lovely Lauren. Beautiful girl, thank you for showing us all how to live life to the fullest. You were smart, brave, fun, feisty and fierce, and knowing you was a pleasure. And you loved my blog, so I know you had truly excellent taste. In the short time you had, I know you did everything right; living unapologetically, doing only what made you happiest and issuing nothing but love and kindness to everyone who knew you. Everyone misses and loves you huge amounts.

#BeMoreLoz

INTRODUCTION

The first thing you should know about me, is that I am not you. A lot more will make sense after that.

Not a direct quote of mine, or even my own words (although I have said all of those words separately, before…). But let's just roll with it, because I've no idea where it came from or who said it before me but it sounds like a pretty good introduction, and I've caught your attention, right?!

For full transparency, I am a cisgender, white, heterosexual woman and this is my account and perspective and from a place I acknowledge to be privileged.

This is somewhat of a biography. A memoir, if you like. But not in the normal, stuffy and official publishing sense. From personal experience, biographies tend to be written (or claim to be written) by celebrities, or those well-known enough to warrant a few hundred thousand followers or fans. For me, unless you count the 4-odd-thousand followers whose interest in my Instagram circles solely on the near-nude pictures of my tits, this is something new. As a British girl in her mid-twenties, I have no connection to the glamorous lifestyles splashed onto the pages of biographies I've previously indulged in (for the most part, while lying in the sun somewhere slightly more exotic than the Oxfordshire towns I've called home for the past decade).

As it is an underlying (or actually, really fucking

obvious) theme throughout this 'memoir', let me start off by telling you that I love sex. I love the heavy breathing, sweaty bodies coming together, climaxing, every-damn-element of sex. I love the passion of it, the pleasure of it, and I think I loved it before I even started doing it.

Chapter 1

Sleeping around is great, providing you know what you're doing.

I really like sex, and I really like McDonald's cheeseburgers, so it's not completely, utterly and entirely shocking that I ended up trading the two, right? Picture this; I am 19, and in a strangers bed after another drunken night out with my girlfriends. Except this one night stand to some degree differed from the rest – I had just traded a night of passion for a 99p morsel of a meal at my local golden arches. At the time, I thought nothing of it. Initially, the accolade had started with a young, hungry and poor teenage girl seeking comfort through the medium of drunk food. Let's blame the tequila for the bargaining tools she then adopted. To this day, the verdict is still out as to whether or not that counts as prostitution…

Hindsight is a beautiful thing. I can only look back and think 'how the fucking fuck did I allow that to happen?' now I've scrutinised and compared then to now. I was doing a lot of hooking up, with a lot of different people. Whilst literally and physically understanding the complications and consequences of my behaviour, emotionally I was not in a place to fully comprehend my actions. If we're friends, then this may well surprise you, but I haven't always been pro-hoe. When I lost my V plates and experienced my first few lovers, I was obsessed with keeping my 'number' as low as possible.

I used to plan one night stands in advance, so I could ensure I re-visited previous partners and make no change to those dreaded digits. As soon as I worked my way through my first few decades, though, I began to change my mind. Having sex is a pretty natural activity, and the way I see it, a craving as necessary to satisfy as those for other luxuries; such as good food and nice wine. I am all for living your life to the very fullest, and denying yourself of what you really want is no way to live it. So I traded in giving a shit what people thought for doing whatever I wanted and having a damn good time.

The cheeseburger barter was a low point, admittedly. I had become so wrapped up in being seen as this sexual siren who could blow like a pro, that I had blurred the boundaries between this and self-respect. Giving myself away to men who didn't deserve or even really want me was not good for my mental state. The cheeseburger purchaser actually went on to publicly shame me some weeks later for being such a 'slut', and brutally picked fun at my looks and weight in front of a lot of people.

I've said it before and I'll say it again; you can't force someone to like or respect you just by sitting on their dick. I learned the hard way, and battled through bouts of depression and loneliness, all the while hating myself and throwing my cat at anyone who looked my way in a vain attempt to feel valued and wanted. It didn't work. I just felt worse.

Sleeping around is great; providing you know what you're doing. I don't mean knowing what goes where and the exact location of the male prostate, but understanding what happens after everyone's happy endings. Whilst mostly a physical act, there are a whole host of psychological outcomes that also go hand in hand with sex.

My early twenties were my 'sexuality treasuring' years. Don't be fooled into thinking I donned a chastity belt and prudish clothing; I was still running around town with my tits out and bedding strangers, but only with careful consideration. I wasn't going home with anyone who wasn't deserving or just for the sake of it. Yes, it became extensively harder to judge this after 134 gin and tonics, but I somehow managed and, as a result, experienced a whole new Nell. A considerable confidence made a home where the self-conscious once lived and I began to understand the true meaning of self-respect. Contrary to popular belief, this, again, does not mean dressing like a nun and shying away from genitalia. Self-respect has nothing to do with nudity or sex. It's just putting yourself first and making choices that make you happy.

I have lost count of how many people I've been with intimately. Not because there are tens of thousands and I can't remember them all (partly true), but because I stopped caring. Your 'number' is exactly that, just a number. No one is defined by how many lovers they've had, and if anyone suggests otherwise, you have my full permission to show them the door. Swiftly, and using your foot as a guide. I don't believe in having regrets, and although some of my past encounters have been less than savoury, they have all contributed in making me, me. I'm sure there used to be some childish saying that if a woman told you her number, you had to multiply it three times to uncover the truth, or something along those lines. Well, I don't know if it's crossed anyone else's minds, but I certainly don't have the time nor patience to multiply and divide the number of people I've slept with in order to deceive people. I hated Maths at school, and I'm categorically not about to learn long division all over again in order to conjure up a more appealing sexual history.

I am well versed in the art that is getting laid. I've had a profusion of experience, but somehow that translates into me being de-valued as a lover. Say, what? Do you mean to tell me that I'm somewhat lacking because I've had more lovers than I have hot drinks? Surely my considerable experience should contribute to me being a more preferential partner, as I've done it all before multiple times and could essentially be described as borderline professional? I'll just leave that with you for pondering.

For the entirety of my life to date, I have been fascinated by sex. I have always yearned to be sexy, and an ambassador for sex. As weird as you may deem it, fourteen-year-old me would spend her babysitting evenings weirdly fascinated by newfound late-night TV shows like *Sexcetera*. Nobody had before told me about these crazy women with glittering body jewellery, miniskirts and no underwear, dancing and laughing and stealing the attention of every male gaze. As a young woman, I gave up my desire to be pretty or cute, but instead, sexy. Sex appeal has always been the most sought after asset for me.

The matriarchs of my family; Grannys, Aunts, Mothers etc, have never been particularly sex positive. We are an overtly sexual family, mind, with none of us shying away from drastic flirtations or innuendos, and I know that the enjoyment of sex is something that we absolutely all have in common. But it's just one of those things never honestly talked about. Not in sober seriousness, anyway. Other than with my sister and cousins, I've never been in a position where I felt comfortable frankly discussing my sex life with a family member. To actually think about this is bizarre. Could you even imagine going to your Gran to fill her in on your latest conquest or seek advice about foreplay? I shudder at the thought. But, why? I know we all love a good boning, so why is it so taboo to express that to those closest to us? It's probably a generational thing and, trust me, I don't want the nitty gritty details of my parent's sex lives, but it just might be nice to have the option to talk about things to someone with a bit more life experience than my close friends.

It's an unfortunate yet unequivocal truth; when it comes to the number of people we've slept with - the higher the number, the higher the judgment. If we can openly brag about who we've rubbed bacons with to our nearest and dearest of pals, why are we always downplaying our sexual history to other people? Why is it that we, mostly women, feel as if we have to conform to the absurd standard society has set for us, and edit personal details about ourselves in order to avoid the risk of other people looking down their noses? Since when did somebody else's opinion matter that much? If you are comfortable within yourself and with your sexuality, and enjoy gland-to-gland combat, providing you are causing no harm to yourself or anyone else, you should take pride in not giving a tiny rat's ass. We should pity the men and other women who choose to pounce on the opportunity, following a woman's revelation of personal details, to use the word 'slut'.

Chapter 2

There is no such thing as a slut.

There is no such thing as a slut. 'Slut' is a made up word, dating back to the 1300's to describe a working class woman. It is a word used to shame, silence and attack women, and, in such a modern age of society, it is unhealthy to obsess over something from the past. And not just the past – ancient fucking history. People are not defined by the amount of sex they do or do not have. Whether your number is closer to 10 or 1,000 - you remain the same person. There is a huge double standard surrounding this. The age old tale of a man being pat on the back for his high number of conquests, whilst women boasting the same number are scorned. Though this is undeniably unfair, slut shaming is a real thing that unfortunately happens all too often.

Do. What. You. Want. I know I already preach it all over the internet until I'm blue in the face, but I will continue to do so until every living, breathing organism has heard me. I have a slightly intimidating, very confident personality which makes some people uneasy – because heaven help us all should a woman be comfortable within herself and speak her mind honestly and unapologetically. I have slept with a fairly large number of people – not millions, but a typically large number, in today's surprisingly small-minded society. I have a body that I love and am proud of, and have no issue showing it off. Trust me, the men in my hometown could draw my boobs from memory. So, what did I do wrong? Which of my actions warranted such vulgar slurs? I made it my priority to stay as safe as I possibly could at all times and made a conscious effort to never knowingly act in a way that could hurt either myself or anyone else. I often had little to no regard for my own feelings, sure, but at the end of the day; I was a single woman doing whatever I wanted. If I wanted to hit the club (can't believe I just wrote that), down half a bottle of their cheapest liquor and stumble into bed with the closest bachelor I could find? Then I fucking did it. And if I fancied snapchatting my nether regions to 37 of my closest friends? I did that too. I can rest easy now, and smile at the prospect of a life with one lover and the same penis forever, knowing that I singled hard enough while I had the opportunity. You'll have good sex, you'll have bad sex and you'll have does-this-even-count-as-sex sex. No regrets.

"I am empowered by my body. I am empowered by my sexuality. I am empowered by feeling comfortable in my skin" – *Kim Kardashian West*

You'll probably even have did-we-even-have-sex sex, circa me in 2014. You know you have those memorable nights that you remember so well because you can't remember anything? Well this is like the hoe version of that. I remember pre-drinking, dancing around my friend's living room and the obligatory pre-night out selfie taking. It was a Friday, I'd had a long week at my first proper job and the outfit I had thought up whilst at work miraculously made me look half decent, and surprisingly not-at-all potato like. If there were ever such a thing as too much White Zinfandel, this is the evening to prove it. I remember so little of the night; possibly only 20 minutes out of a four hour evening and the memories that I do have are blurred visuals of wildly throwing my limbs around the dance floor, queueing up for another shot and snogging my girlfriend underneath the smoking area's staircase. I don't remember going home with a boy, but I do remember him entering me at some point, and being perplexed at how frighteningly erect his quiff was.

And, yes, I do mean quiff.

I then recall stumbling around in the very early hours, having left him sleeping, trying to find myself a ride home. After what seemed like a lifetime searching, it was a taxi ride that I will be eternally thankful for, and getting home and into bed with my bestie that night had never felt so good. A number of months later, one of my Tinder matches popped up and asked me out. I engaged in conversation and we wound up discussing the pending date. He then told me he was looking forward to seeing me again. I was stopped dead in my tracks. He went on to mention how much fun I was, and how rare it was to meet a girl so willing to engage in spanking and butt stuff with a chap she'd just met. Memory serving me correctly, I had never met this particular boy before, let alone ridden him into the sunrise. Yeah, I was wrong. And, yeah, he was boyo with the tall hair. Told you I was good, though.

I have no doubts in claiming that most women in today's society have been labelled as a slut. It's painful, and it has a tendency to stick with you. If anyone knows, it's me. The sexual landscape of our world and particular generation have been steadily moving and evolving for quite some time now and, at this point, sex and dating are on mutually ambiguous terms. People are having more sex on the first date, sex without dating, before they even start dating, and casual partners and hook-ups are becoming increasingly common around most of the world. I'm not arguing that it is within every human's interests to be going out and doing the deed with every other person they meet, but a lot of people enjoy a bit of the old in and out - whether or not they're in a committed relationship.

So, am I unclean and impure for sleeping with a lot of people? If two consensual adults decide to have sex, it's important to notice that there are in fact two people involved, and if one of them is immediately going to shame the other afterward, then that person has a clear misunderstanding of fucking in the 21st century. With today's contraceptives and general knowledge of human anatomy, there is absolutely no reason why women should be seen as any different to men when it comes to being sexually active.

Society puts so much pressure on sex as both the be-all and the end-all, and this pressure is increased exponentially for women. We should be virginal, but still sexy, the girl next door and the femme fatale, 'a lady in the street and a freak in the sheets'. There is so much pressure to put out and have sex - and also not have it - that it's no wonder that women grow up disenchanted and confused about their sexuality. There is no such thing as an experienced virgin, and yet that is what we, as women, are expected to be. I know many, many women who enjoy casual sex with multiple partners. I did it for ages! From coming into contact with these women over the last 20 years, I can tell you for sure that nobody fits a sexual stereotype. Sexual stereotypes simply do not exist. They were fabricated to sustain and perpetuate a little power structure called patriarchy, and it's no secret that this structure leaves no room for diverse realities.

WOMAN UP

Chapter 3

Let's talk about sex and all of her brothers and sisters like they ain't no thing because, really, they ain't.

As I write this, I'm now in my 25th year. Do save your age concerns and experience criticism until the end. I am still young and, granted, I'm not stereotypically old enough to write an entire book dedicated to my life in sex and sex positivity, but you'll soon learn that I've got enough experience under my belt to dedicate a series of novels to the cause.

I believe myself to be completely sex positive. I am passionate about starting and carrying the sex positive movement. Come and find me if you're pro sex and against slut shaming, and we'll start the official club tomorrow. The world needs more of us actively being reasonable towards women's sexuality, and that's final. Give calling us sluts and whores a rest, and learn to respect the empowerment and owning of one's own body. And just to make sure y'all are on the same page (figuratively) – being sex positive does not translate into telling every man and his dog about your sex life and preferences. That's my job. Sex positivity doesn't mean that you are owed anything. Sex positivity is not an excuse for wandering hands, catcalling or touching people without consent. Get your hand off my arse and your arm off my shoulder; I believe in the right to consent, which doesn't mean you can touch uninvited.

Sex is pretty much my life. I know that sounds awfully one dimensional and like the opening to a guidebook for nymphomaniacs, but it is. I owe so much to sex. And I just want talking about it to be as normal as talking about the weather when you run into your neighbour putting their recycling bins out. And, again, this doesn't necessarily mean chatting casually about full on shagging; but everything that goes alongside it, too. I'm calling for full open-ness on body positivity, shaming, sexual health and safety, periods and puberty and human relationships.

Sex means so much to me that, when faced with a near death experience and the sudden flash of my short and alarmingly sausage-shaped life before my eyes, I made peace with God's wishes, given that he had ensured my time was spent doing what I most enjoyed. To cut a long story short, I over exerted myself whilst mid-deep throat, gagged and choked on my own vomit. But after a glass of water and some panicked panting whilst laying on the bathroom floor, calling out for my Y shaped coffin, I was miraculously saved. You know what they say - live by the sword, die by the sword.

Standing up for sex means normalising those

'forbidden' subjects rarely touched on. Rape culture needs to die a quick and painful death. So do me a favour and make the next 70-odd thousand words worthwhile by ensuring you're telling people that rape is never a debate. It's right or wrong, consensual or assault and absolutely never at the fault of the victim. People know that rape is wrong, surely?! I cannot bear the thought of living in a world where people are confused as to whether or not they are allowed to force themselves upon someone else. I think it's known, and people are scared to speak out so as not to offend the misogynistic wankers in various aspects of power around the world. Well, now is the time to speak up and speak out; we are all in this together.

Despite being rather infatuated with sex and the idea of being and having it; I grew up in a small-minded village, with little to no open and honest discussions about sex. At all. My severe lack of knowledge juxtaposed with my desire for the unknown fuelled confusing but consequentially 'frigid' (not self-labelled) early teenage years. At ten years old, I had my first kiss. I was understandably overcome with passion having just watched Aaron Samuels and Cady Heron get it on in *Mean Girls*. Well, sort of, anyway; we were writhing around on his bottom bunk, neither of us with even a hint of an idea about what we were doing. It was pretty gross in all honesty – tongues all over the shop. After that, I didn't dabble in much tonsil tennis until my first clubbing experience half a dozen years later. Naturally,

I was irresistible in my low-rise, sequin miniskirt and velvet ankle boots, paired with a side fringe that started somewhere south of my ear.

While I avoided locking lips with any potential suitors, I was a completely different person post first kiss. I began to notice boys, and I mean really notice them. I was crowned 'kiss chase' winner more often than anyone else, after perfecting the act of sprinting around a playground launching myself and my pursed lips at my squealing peers. High school was somewhat of a gateway for my pending sexuality. I had started to grow myself some itty bitty titties, and I'd even suffered my first monthly bleed. So, not only was I on the cusp of being a true adulting credit to society, but also stuffed the front pocket of my school backpack full of hundreds of sanitary towels of every size and absorbency every morning. You know, just in case every other woman in school attendance had the painters in at the same time, or in case anybody ran out of pillows at a sleepover. Most of the boys in my year group had joined from other schools and had a wider and far more mature sexual knowledge than I did, teaching me lifelong lessons that I'll carry with me to my grave. Before I entered my secondary years, I was still under the impression that a blow job meant blowing air into someone's bum hole. Seriously.

I started high school at age 12 (not a girl, but definitely not yet a woman) and was immediately exposed to the sexually explicit answers of the questions I had been asking myself. A far cry from what I was used to – sitting at the back of the swimming club bus, giggling over the mere thought of the male species, and gagging over the girl who witnessed her parents snogging in the kitchen. Not only did my primary school Sex Education teach me almost nothing, but the information I did take away from it was almost all incorrect. Picture a group of 30-odd children around the tender age of ten, herded together in the makeshift school library (a tiny room possessing migraine-inducing curtains and a full collection of ancient encyclopaedias). The curtains are drawn because God forbid the sunlight distract us from the birds and the bees, and the carpet is hard and bears a similar texture to my bikini line three days post shave. After a brief and frighteningly un-detailed introduction, the television is rolled into the room, the video tape wound back to the beginning, and the 'learning' begins.

I know it has been a considerable while since my school days, but I would be more than a little surprised to discover that many of the sex ed rituals have drastically changed. I mean, are you even learning about the journey of reproduction if it isn't via a video, taped in the early 1980s? To summarize this riveting motion picture, a heterosexual married couple (with fairly questionable hairstyles) take some form of straight-legged missionary position (spoiler alert: this position is highly uncomfortable, not at all sexy and almost impossible to maintain) and slowly rub against each other. In truth, you see nothing other than a starched duvet cover ascending and descending at a glacial pace. No noise, no mess and no reality. And this is pretty much how I thought sex was for the next few years - creating friction as you lie on top of each other, doing your best ironing board impression. I didn't know that things went inside other things and that those things then leak, make babies and make you poorly downstairs. Fertilised was a way that my mum had never offered my eggs be cooked before.

Teaching both our sons and daughters about sexual assault, sexually transmitted infections, contraception and the workings of the human body should be compulsory learning. I am willing to stake my next month's wage on the fact that it would come into practice a lot more in adult life than Pythagoras' theorem ever would. Sex Education should feature anal, oral and vaginal sex. It should touch on the workings of relationships and the meaning of rape culture. They should learn of emotions, what they mean and how to deal with them. I would honestly be a much more favourable human being should I have learned at a sensible age the meaning of emotions like rage, grief, heartbreak and, most importantly, hanger.

Chapter 4

Anything you can do, I can do bleeding.

I was ill prepared and had absolutely no idea about the world that awaited me. The word clueless would be lost in describing pre-pubescent me. Nobody told me about tampons (queue the most awkward teacher-student moment ever on a school trip in 2007), and, other than the diagram of the 1970's pubic topiary (which subconsciously I seem to have based my look on), I wasn't prepared for the premiere of the hairs that appeared on my legs, armpits and stomach in my early teens. The majority of STIs were missed off the teaching check list that day, and the only mention of contraception was a demonstration using a sealed condom packet.

We millennials are a generation raised in the glow of online pornography. Owing to our lacklustre and disappointing sex education, it's almost the norm for us to automatically seek out porn sites to fill in the blanks left by subpar sex ed. The only problem here, is that porn is stereotypically designed to mirror a male gaze. Well, mainstream porn, anyway. All too often, this propagates unrealistic ideas of sex, and especially how it should look and feel. I do not recommend watching anything with 'fisting, orgy or hardcore' in the title for your first time. Curiosity is healthy and encouraged, but researching further than Google's top three porn hits will provide more of an accurate representation and honest answers to any questions you might be plagued with.

On a side note, why don't we have better named pornos? Don't get me wrong, there are times in life where the only thing that will satisfy one's appetite is 'busty Brazilian creampie compilation version 3', and I am well aware of fem-porn and all of the sites and videos specifically tailored for a woman's viewing, but they are never named adequately. I struggle to be enticed by the objectification of women as sex objects. Considering my mood the majority of the time (tired and irritable but always with a hint of horny) I'd like to see a page full of clips with titles like 'gorgeous brunette with a high IQ and great job beds Tinder match after four great dates' and 'hilarious 25-year old with 4,000 Instagram followers finally meets a man willing to put in enough time and effort to give her multiple orgasms'.

We need to up our Sex Ed game, and ensure people are really learning about sexual health. They should know how to insert a tampon and, if they don't want to, the other options that they can use instead. I discovered menstrual cups when I was 21. 21! Eight years of bleeding and believing the only solution to be a wad of compressed cotton on a string. The generations below us should be taught about what causes infections and how best to avoid or treat them. Take it from someone who thought their vagina was actually going to dissolve and drop off the first time they contracted thrush.

I've had chlamydia twice. Partially because I wasn't aware of the symptoms, and the fact that there are nearly almost none, and partially because I kept having unprotected sex with wanky rugby players who were undoubtedly also bedding the rest of West London. Not only are we seldom taught the range of sexually transmitted infections and diseases and the extent of their symptoms and side effects, but those that are known of carry a reputation of shame and embarrassment. They are a part of sex and human life - stop giving them such negative connotations.

There is also an assumption that they tend to go hand in hand with being sexually promiscuous. Whilst the chances of contagion are higher when you're sleeping with more people, you can contract an STI from your first, third or 75th lover. You can get herpes from your first kiss. Viruses like HPV can even be passed when losing your virginity to a steady partner. These illnesses don't discriminate based on social constructs. Contracting an STI or STD is nothing to do with a lack of judgement or poor morals; they can happen to anyone.

Those that are transmitted sexually are no different

than any other illness. The only reason they're treated as such is because of puritanical beliefs about sexuality. Considering how sex-saturated our society is, it seems incredibly hypocritical that one can be shamed and degraded for participating in sex and subsequently getting an unwanted infection or disease from it. It's important to stay safe, granted, but nobody made jokes at your expense when you got the flu from your little sister Katie. Whilst I don't doubt the passing of germs is done entirely differently when it comes down to STIs, the principal is the same. It is bad luck and weak immune systems you want to be blaming.

It's not just the jokes that need to disappear. Even the official language that is used to describe our sexual health status can be problematic. When we are STI/D free, we are said to be 'clean', implying that those who do live with them are 'dirty'. Not only is it important to openly and honestly discuss these infections, but equally we must be conscious of the language we use in these dialogues. STIs have notoriously fallen victim to bad branding. For example, did you know that the word 'herpes' derives from a Greek word that means to creep or crawl? And the translation of 'syphilis' is 'swine love'.

STI stigma actually perpetuates slut shaming. Obviously, the call to end shaming of any kind has been hollered through town and city worldwide, but we still need to continue to present the message that having sex is OK, and so is the burden of any unwanted consequences. Sure, it's unideal and almost never comes at an appropriate time when you're giving your genitals a couple of months of R&R, but it's something that should be dealt with maturely and professionally. You're not a bad person if you got the clap because you did the dirty with a club promoter in a Magaluf public toilet. I want to see Holly and Phil on that uncomfortable looking sofa, educating their daytime viewers about these things, in between bouts of Gino's carbonara and flirting with Gok Wan. In doing so, we might even stop the cycle of some of the more widely distributed infections. Think about it; the more comfortable we are talking about it, the more likely we are to share the detail with our potential lover – eliminating the risk of spreading the infection further than necessary.

So, let's break the mould. Let's talk about sex and all of her brothers and sisters like they ain't no thing because, really, they ain't. I actively encourage the talking of subjects which may be deemed 'taboo'. My number one party starting fave? Your period. I rattle on about mine all the time, in the hope that other women and the men around me notice that, woah, hey, this is actually totally normal and OK to discuss. Let's get the message that talking about your period is OK across to the entire world, and most notably to the straight boys stuck behind their computer keyboards.

Fact of the day – once a month, every month, most women (and those with a womb) bleed.

Sometimes for one or two days, sometimes for over a week. It is our uterus' version of a friendly reminder are not pregnant. Almost like one of those really loud and annoying ringing alarm clocks - except it is all day and all night for an extended period of time, and no amount of bouncing your uterus on its head or smashing it against the wall will stop it. I honestly believe that men have some sort of warped sense of reality, and believe it to be pleasurable for us to literally haemorrhage from the fanny every four weeks. Quelle surprise! It's shit. We don't get a choice in the matter; we can't tick a magic box and unsubscribe from our menstrual cycle. It would be a luxury to laugh, sneeze or clear my throat without it resulting in an instant tsunami of blood leaving my vagina.

As opposed to the feminine hygiene product commercials, a period is actually a mini-break to Hell where you are crippled with pain and debt from buying a handful of tampons, rather than the flowery, smiling experience you see during the ad break. According to the advert, I should be fit to run a marathon following the insertion of my new best-ever tampon. *Reality check* - it's a big deal if I'm vertical for more than six hours whilst I'm surfing the crimson wave. And, whilst we're on the subject, 'PMS' isn't an excuse for boys to use when they piss their girlfriends off; it's an all-consuming rage, a weeping declaration of love, a hoard of unnecessary and unwanted zits and an uncontrollable urge to dip everything in chocolate. Pre-Menstrual syndrome? More like Please Make me S'mores.

Women know when their period has started, we

just don't necessarily know in advance when it's going to start. Or finish, for that matter. Queue the endless stream of ruined sheets, underwear and pyjama bottoms. Regardless of how prepared you are in the lead up to the big blood spill, you can almost guarantee that Aunt Flo will pay her visit the one day you opted for a pale pink, silky thong rather than your dark 'safe' undies.

In truth, 'chasing the cotton mouse' is a term far too endearing to accurately describe perioding. Unless its ultra slim, having a compressed pad of cotton the width of a marker pen shoved up our lady passage is uncomfortable as fuck. The image of a naïve and 14-year-old me physically waddling around after the insertion of her first plus-sized tampon is hard to shake. Regardless of the size of the tampon or how tight and toned your pelvic floor is, those long-tailed devils have a fun habit of squeezing themselves free. Either when at full capacity or, more commonly, when we take a poop.

THIS is reality. And pads? Grossest invention ever. It's the grown woman's answer to a nappy and essentially means we stew in our own blood for hours. Oh, and the strange winged design means it more often than not gets stuck and rips out half our pubes. Top tip – if you want to scare a boy away, pull out a tampon and throw it at him. Hell hath no fear like a man-child faced with a tampon. (If he's really pissed you off, try pulling the tampon straight from your lady garden as opposed to your handbag).

What's worse (than actually leaking blood once a

month) is when men refuse to stick their dick anywhere near it, because it's 'gross' and displeasing to their fragile, fragile masculinity. There's never a resounding 'thanks that we've managed not to let you knock us up', just a sexist, inequitable dismissal. And you know what's way more gross than a little period blood? The shit stains you leave in the toilet bowl, the hair you block our shower drains with and the sticky white fluid that you expect us to gratefully receive on our bare bodies. Oh shit, yeah, and you try and make us swallow it. THAT is gross.

We should be able to talk about periods. As in, not in the privacy of a girl's WhatsApp group and without fear of reaction. Because it is more than normal. In fact, it is so normal, it's comparable to being worried about discussing cheese sandwiches. Unheard of, right?

Being a woman is tough shit. I stand for any corporation who allow for menstrual time off work. And, whilst sometimes I need a day or two to cradle my hot water bottle, binge watch *Grey's Anatomy* and stuff my face with leftover pasta bake, more often than not I am living and succeeding – just as I would any other day of the month. My period doesn't make me weak (oh, pleeeease, have you ever witnessed man-flu?) – it makes me strong as hell. Because I get up, sort my shit out and get on with my life, despite the tiny crime scene in my pants. Anything you can do, I can do bleeding.

Chapter 5

The further adventures of my chocolate starfish and I.

I don't believe in having regrets but, if I did, it would be not insisting on more informative sex education. I'm almost certain that if I did, my first chance meeting with anal sex would have run a lot smoother. No, I didn't know when it was going to happen but, had I had the necessary sex education, I wouldn't have needed to. Having experienced such a frightful encounter first hand and such opportunity repeatedly popping up since, I have essentially perfected the art of anal. To achieve perfect, pain-free bumming, it is essential that you are lube-happy. Without it, you'll be up shit creek – literally.

Generally speaking, nipping down the back passage is not immediately what springs to mind when imagining mutually pleasurable activities to partake in with a partner. Is anal sex an act you'd class as intimate? It's often just seen as something that men seek because they've seen it in a porno/heard it's a little tighter. Either that or because of the bragging rights it'll give them 3 pints in on a Friday night.

I remember watching a really old *Misfits* episode (when it first came out) when I was in my mid-teens, and one of the characters was shagging a woman who only took it in the butt. I thought it was the most bizarre thing, because why on earth would you let anything go up there the wrong way, right? I convinced myself that it was purely an exit route and not to be confused for an entrance. Anal sex was something that even I frowned upon until my later teenage years. When discussing the subject with my mother on what I've now deemed 'anal Wednesday', she seemed horrified at first, but then shrugged it off and continued with what she was doing. So what changed everyone's opinions on this subject? Perhaps it was the dawn of programmes such as *Sex and the City*. Samantha is often more than enthusiastic to partake in a little bumming and I would be willing to bet at least twenty pence (I'm not made of money, you know) that most of you have either experimented with butt stuff, thought about butt stuff or experienced accidental 'wrong hole' slippage.

Doesn't it seem high time we all stopped being so embarrassed or squeamish about the topic of taking it in the hoop, or simply pretending it doesn't exist? There should be no shame in enjoying a little butt lovin' every now and then, if you are so inclined. Anal remains one of the most misunderstood 'hobbies' to date. I've come across many a man in my time who was reduced to climax and ejaculation within seconds of their partner slipping a digit, and it's far more common than you'd realise. The male 'g-spot' is situated in the prostate, and can only be felt internally and through the anus. I also happen to know many a woman who partakes in sodomy, whether the river be running red or not. Unlike vaginal sex, it is not considered a natural process, although studies have suggested the first participants dated back to the ancient Greeks, based on their intimate pottery designs. Can you imagine if we still made art in this way? Someone hit up Tracey Emin and request she makes some soup bowls decorated only with illustrations of housewives giving their husbands one off the wrist whilst they watch *Panorama*. Successful anal takes a considerable amount of practice and patience.

Anal has been perceived as a taboo for such a long time because, as mentioned, it technically is an exit route. It's seen as 'gay sex' and we all know how absurdly ridiculous some of society are about homosexuality, or any sexual inclination other than that for someone of an opposite sex. In this day and age, however, where sex is more prominent than ever and a 'vajazzle' is seen as old, vanilla news, the shock factor doesn't often come into play. Much like discussing sex as a whole, this is likely generational and I don't advise asking your great uncle Norman how much anal sex he had in his heyday. For their generation, sex is something to be had in private and only discussed in hushed tones. I'm almost certain that while in public, the older generation may have scorned at a little bum fun, behind closed doors they were knee deep in KY Jelly - a little disturbing to imagine but I'm sure you catch my drift. Over the last twenty years, the addition of anal sex into relationships in the United States has increased from 25% to 40% - so perhaps my fellow butt lovers and I are onto something? Still, many societies have a stigma against this kind of intercourse for religious or personal reasons.

I've had some bad anal in my time, believe you me. There's nothing more disappointing than rubbish sex, particularly when it's experimenting with something different. It's a bummer - literally. Anal is arguably an art form, something that you have to perfect and something never to be rushed into. Plus, it only really works when you're doing it right. Taking your time and making sure you are constantly on mutual levels of pleasure is the way to achieve that passionate vibe. One wrong move and you could really be in the shit - again, literally. You've been warned. So is anal sex a deal breaker? You wouldn't break up with a partner because they refused to invite you in through the back door, would you? Apparently, anal is the new oral - so would you consider terminating your relationship because they wouldn't go downtown? I'm unconvinced.

I had anal sex for the first time when I was 18 (prior to that I had experienced a few accidentally on purpose 'slips', but it's hard to count them when my only reaction was to scream at them to remove said item from my bottom, immediately). It did not feel good. Perhaps because he fucked like he danced; sporadically, only for four minutes at a time and with no sense of rhythm, but also because he aimlessly thrust into me with no cautionary tale, lubrication or preparation. Long story short, it did not end how you'd want it to end - neither the anal sex or the relationship. Fear not though friends, almost every bout of anal I have endured since then has been performed correctly and to my liking, and was nothing less than pleasurable. Once, of course, you've gotten over the feeling that you could actually be pooing backwards.

Essentially, anal is no longer a taboo. It has become something that the majority of us are now comfortable talking about, even before a glass of wine. So, before society changes its mind and reverts back to hoop-hating hell - embrace that pretty little rose bud. Entry is not something to be forced, however, and if anal is not your cup of tea then don't fret - it's definitely not compulsory! I still stand in my opinion that good old-fashioned cock-in-fanny sex is better for me – so perhaps anal is just the special occasion sex for us hetero types. "Merry Christmas, fuck me in my ass!" I think that could catch on...

As with almost everything, it really is about what you make it. Taking your time and making sure you are constantly on mutual levels of pleasure is the clear way to achieve a more passionate vibe. Arguably, anal sex could be more passionate than vaginal, considering it's such an intimate and personal area and not somewhere that people venture often. Like losing your virginity, the first time is always going to be a little uncomfortable. Over time the feelings experienced should grow more intense and pleasurable. And I really mean over time - it's rare that you'll develop a love for butt stuff overnight.

The most important thing to remember is to be completely relaxed. Foreplay is always key. Like my dance teacher used to chant in my ear three times a week; "stretch it out". Once you are fully relaxed (play some Joni Mitchell, or something), and have let go of all thoughts, fears and 'what if I shit on them' worries, then you are on your way. Protection is wise. Always. From both strange penises and bears. Personally, if my partner has requested to enter my exit then I like to be completely in control. Reverse Cowgirl allows for a lot more movement and control than your standard bending over. *Bonus point* - this position means your partner won't have a full view of your 'there's a foreign object in my arsehole' face. This is just something I've picked up from the further adventures of my chocolate starfish and I – personal preference is always key in all aspects of sex, so make sure you're comfortable. Once again (for those of you skimming through this particular chapter), anal ain't for everyone. Much like all other sexual activity, there's no shame in not being into it. Do your own thing. Just don't force yourself or anyone else to do something that you'd really rather not.

Chapter 6

Lord only knows how children of early teenage years have a full and complex understanding of what it is to have butt sex when all we'd been taught in school was that puberty starts when you find hairs in your armpits.

I don't really remember when I first heard about anal sex, although I am fairly certain it came from the mouths of 13 year old boys in my French class. Lord only knows how children of early teenage years have a full and complex understanding of what it is to have butt sex when all we'd been taught in school was that puberty starts when you find hairs in your armpits.

The boys I encountered at school taught me almost everything I know. And, honestly, it was pretty daunting. I was never popular, and having this knowledge and maturity made most of my schoolmates deem themselves as better than me, leaving me as the butt of most of their jokes. I found myself more often than not, sat in maths class avoiding the jeers and taunts of the boys and girls who branded me 'frigid'. Told you I didn't self label. I had a penchant for powder blue eyeshadow and thick sweater vests while the other girls wore bright lipstick and short skirts, showing off smooth, tan legs. I was so desperate to be 'cool' like them. They seemed so grown up and as if they could catch the attention of anyone they wanted.

I tried in vain to fit in with said cool kids. Much to the dismay of my poor parents, teachers and homework grades, this meant hours spent on MSN the minute I dismounted the school bus. I developed several different crushes on several different boys (not for the last time), meaning my notepad was never free of heart-shaped doodles and confessions of my 'great' loves. Ultimately, I settled on one particular chap and focused all my obsession and attention on him. To this day, I know he secretly liked me back. But, regardless, my unpopular status meant our relationship was confined to late night webcam sessions and occasional and fleeting eye contact during third period history. Over time (a week or two, max), my feelings grew stronger and, naturally, I took the liaison to the next step… Direct translation: me stealing my mother's lingerie and parading it on webcam for the weekly fifteen minutes that I was home alone for.

The years passed and I began to rule the school. Joking, I spent my lunchtimes cowering behind the pasta bar. I befriended a group of like-minded girls, and we did almost everything together. Sadly, by this I mean waiting outside the library doors every break time, waiting for it to open so we could perform our daily ritual of reading each other shark attack stories and crawling around on all fours pretending to be cats. Ah, to be a tween again.

Irrespective of my seeming unpopularity, word got out about my out of hours webcam antics and I was taunted for that. I was grateful, really. I've never been one to shy away from publicity, no matter how negative – there's no such thing, didn't you know? Plus it bagged me some private internet time with my newest fascination; a bleach blonde, Jack Wills clad (remember when that was cool?!) rugby player two school years above me. I was convinced he was the one, until a month into our 'relationship' when he called it off because I was 'creepy'. Apparently, confessing your undying love for someone who you've never actually spoken to in person is a little off-putting. Who'd have thought! Queue a week of sleepless nights spent wrapped like a burrito in my duvet listening to Kelly Clarkson on repeat and wailing into a pillow. It was all very 90's movie, clichéd teen angst.

Regardless of how crazy he thought I was, he came crawling back for more (I can't be certain, but I would be willing to put a wager on this being down to my excellent feline impersonations) and introduced me to the wild world of sexting. I was due to move 400 miles south a few weeks later (as a result of my 'out of control, overtly sexual behaviour', or something) and so obviously I offered him a parting gesture – my virginity.

Sadly, as I was only 14 and dear old ma and pa were fluent in authoritarian-style parenting, my phone was confiscated at 9pm sharp every night prior to my bed going and bad boys with blonde hair were strictly off limits.

One fateful morning, I woke to find my beloved mobile had been unlocked during the night and, to my absolute horror, all texts from Bleach Blonde and therefore rigorously confidential plans regarding the baking of my first love custard were common knowledge to my furious parents. I was in a lot of trouble, and was forbidden to leave the house for any reason other than schooling. The hardest punishment of all, however? Despite my hordes of desperate texts and jaunty-angled pictures of my B cups, it was at least six months before I heard from my pale-haired love again. Turns out my ever-so-slightly over-bearing and over-protective father had his own private words with the king of bleach, warning him off me and reducing the 16-year-old to tears. It wasn't the first and definitely wasn't to be the last of the mortifying acts he would perform in my honour.

Chapter 7

There's only so much 75-year-old scrotum a 21-year-old girl can take. And it's none.

The age of consent has been made so for a reason. I would rather give up fish finger sandwiches for life than admit it, but I am so lucky and eternally thankful that my parents intervened. Whilst at the time, their calling my potential hymen-breaker and dismantling any hope of a relationship between the two of us almost made me a runaway, I now fully understand and completely appreciate their efforts. I was a child. No 14-year-old is emotionally stable enough or ready to embark on a serious sexual relationship. I was stupid, immature and, looking back, it's a worry how determined I was. All because some of my friends had started moonlighting as booty calls. Guess what? It isn't even a big deal. Virginity is a social construct created to shame women into having sex. Oh, and then when you finally do it – you're shamed for that too.

I didn't get to be a runaway. Nothing more than packing an old camping rucksack at age 9 and hiding behind the car (on the driveway) for half an hour, anyway. I was shipped off to England, and had somewhat of a hard time letting go of my past life. I now found myself attending a small all-girls' Catholic school close to central Oxford. The girls were friendly, albeit frighteningly naïve, and the toxic potion of my pent-up anger towards the world (especially my parents) and broad new knowledge of all things adult led me into a position of hierarchy. A sort of Regina George figure, albeit slightly chubbier, sporting eyeliner to rival that of Miss Winehouse, hair back-combed within an inch of its life and constant fondness for talking about sex. I was fearless. Much like Regina, I'm not confident that any of my 'friends' actually liked me, or if they were just terrified into pretending to. School hours often found me playing dubstep in a room full of revising A-Level students. Not a genre I'm particularly drawn to but it was far from the classics they were used to and totally cool, right?

It took only a handful of guesses before I figured out multiple staff member's computer log ins and used up their allotted internet allowance playing a variety of PornHub's finest for my wide-eyed classmates. The practice of only spending time with girls made me thirsty for any form of male attention. Plus I always needed another chance to show my apparently innocent classmates how bad-ass I was. I had no issue flaunting my verging on neon orange legs, and I rolled the waistband of my skirt so many times, it would have been considered a fashionable belt in the 1980's. That was until my parents received a phone call home from the deputy head who, along with the band of other teachers dining in the canteen, became privy to my actual arsehole as I leant over the salad bar one pivotal lunch time (it was the last time I opted for the healthy option, I can assure you).

In desperate pursuit of attention and with the aspiration to show the rest of the school how much of a sexual temptress I was, I openly flirted with the only eligible, young male teacher in school; and it soon became no secret that he was the object of my desire. I took things to a new level, however, when workmen were called to fix a leak in the sport's hall's roof. I could barely contain myself – there was fresh meat on the territory, for crying out loud, and this was an opportunity asking to be milked for the reputation I so desperately sought after. So, much to even my friend's astonishment, I seized our regular lunch time sunbathing spot on the lawn, and rid myself of my bra. That's right, I was not yet 16 and sunbathing topless mere metres away from not only a group of dis-believing builders, but my ever terrifying ex-nun headmistress's office. And yes, I was asked to leave within the next year.

Having moved to London almost five years later, said male teacher and I found the time to 'catch up' once again. We met at a local pub, reminisced on the good ol' days, and discussed how much our lives had changed. Admittedly, I probably fancied him more when I was fifteen and he was the scandalously desirable teacher that almost everyone in the class was fawning over. But the excitement was exactly the same. I felt like we had sky-rocketed back in time and I was looking at him in awe through my combed over side fringe and heavily mascara clad lashes. When he kissed me I could taste the envy of the other girls in my class, and had that kind of 'probably should hide somewhere because this is illegal' sensation. Looking back, I can't tell whether it was the seventeen glasses of Rose or that naughty school girl feeling but, following his offer of a bed for the night, I politely declined and walked myself home. Oh, and I couldn't for the life of me stop calling him 'Sir'. Maybe that was my downfall…

The teacher was my first, but by no means last whirl with a partner in a position of power. Power is sexy, and that's no secret. I've fancied almost all of my bosses thus far (other than she who was dating my father). Because, the short of the story is; I like being told what to do, but only in the bedroom.

I've never really dated men my own age. I find with the increase in years on earth, comes the increase in sexual experience and maturity. In short, they're less likely to ask you where your clitoris is. In my last few years as a scholar, I dabbled once or twice with boys of a similar age, but this mostly entailed sitting next to each other on the bus to school and getting fingered by one of them at a pool party. I am mature for my age, and I don't have the energy or the goddamn patience to mother my boyfriends. Get your shit together, figure out what you want to do and then talk to me about my plans next Friday night. The invitation to 'chill' has never enticed me. I'm a grown ass woman, and what time I have to chill, I like to spend alone, with Netflix and a powerful vibrator. Ask me out! I like steak.

I can remember the first celebrity I ever fancied. And, despite my at the time incessant printing of his headshots, it is one I rarely talk about. Mostly because the mere thought of him cringes me to my very core. Given that I was only just pushing double digits (age wise, in this context) and he must have been somewhere in his sixties at the time. Rather sadly, he recently passed away and so I would like to take a moment, now, to remember him. So thank you, Dirty Den from EastEnders, for birthing my love for unseemly older men.

It's no wonder that I've often opted for the silver fox. I think this is probably a result of my long term craving to be the most adventurous sex pixie to ever bend over and delve into the unknown. I just happened to pair said desperation with excellent taste in men, and found myself teamed up with some serious genetic triumphs. When residing in the big smoke, I even went as far as joining specific sugar daddy dating sites. That didn't work out. I gave a few of them a chance and, despite how desperate I was to have my television licence paid for, there's only so much 75-year-old scrotum a 21-year-old girl can take. And it's none. Older men are just generally better, though. They are less likely to behave like a prat, and definitely less likely to still have the same Spiderman themed bedroom that they did when they were twelve. I can officially declare that no man of maturity has ever left me buying his drinks in Vodka Revs whilst he chain smoked and had the club photographer take photos from multiple angles of him and his equally man-child like friends. When courting older men, I've never been ditched last minute on a Friday night because the football is on, and my date has forgotten how to practice self-control, and subsequently enjoyed too many lagers to drive. Personally, I've just always found something more attractive in the older man; most notably, the ability not to laugh at their own farts.

Chapter 8

If you're hot and single, you'd better believe I'm going to spark an interest. Irrespective of your age being more than double mine.

I have had but one full sexual encounter with someone younger. It was on a mini break with one of my girlfriends, and we were staying with her brother at his university accommodation. 'Mini Break' is a term used loosely in this case; whilst you may be picturing four poster beds and walks on a beach, it was much more Aldi vodka and the scarring image of sweaty teens gurning and grinding on each other in-between rounds of £1 shots. Regardless, post coitus and after rolling around his university halls in my knickers at 4am, I was considerably mortified. I couldn't get to grips with the fact that I'd allowed a younger man to physically enter my shrine to all that is adult and mature. I mean, I was most likely still drunk and over-reacting hideously because he was only a year younger than me, but it just shows that personal preference reigns, as always. Even more embarrassing, perhaps, is when I got over the initial shock and realised how bloody gorgeous he was. I texted him once or twice, and he ghosted me. Shameful.

It's no top secret that many women favour a younger man – more commonly referred to as the 'toy boy' and without the unwarranted 'Mrs Robinson' subtext, if you please. It's not for me, but I totally get the attraction. For an older woman, to be shown interest by a younger man must be exciting and a real boost to the ego. From experience, I concur. Reportedly, sexual attentiveness and the ability to get and stay aroused can actually decrease for men as they increase in age. So, if she's not getting it from her middle-aged husband, is she wrong to leave him for a twenty-something in his sexual prime? Sometimes you've just gotta do what you've gotta do. Somewhat staggeringly, 16% of relationships in France are now between an older woman and a younger man (the current French President's wife is actually 24 years his senior), with the stat thought to increase over the next decade. Ooh La La! Allegedly, they believe that embracing a man their junior keeps life more interesting. Can't argue with that now, can you?

There are a plethora of celebrities with much-younger other halves. When Cheryl Cole announced that she was pregnant with Liam Payne's baby, people really lost their shit over it. She's only ten years his senior but they initially met when he was just 14. Bearing in mind he was an X Factor contestant and she was a judge, they hardly leapt into each other's knickers from day dot. But it was something the British public just couldn't wrap their heads around – claiming she was a 'cougar' when she fell pregnant at 33. To be in the public eye 24/7 must be hard enough, but to have them document every relationship, every affair and every heartbreak must be devastating. And, guaranteed, all those spending their days fretting over the trials and tribulations of various celebrity relationships must have also previously been witness to the rest of their lives and previous relationships or breakups. So, because a woman is a little older than her current boyfriend or baby daddy, we shouldn't allow her the opportunity to be happy? I'm not so sure this theory would stand in court…

If you haven't watched the entire *Desperate Housewives* box set multiple times then we probably aren't close friends, but one of the premier storylines throughout the first few series was the affair that gorgeous, glamorous, recently retired model Gaby Solis embarked upon with John Rowland, her teenage gardener. Inevitably, she was a bored housewife neglected by her career and money obsessed husband and desperate for attention and affection. But he was young, naïve and a virgin; and, obviously (in classic noughties sitcom style), he fell madly in love with her. She ended up breaking his heart.

Many ladies claim that a younger lover or more youthful life partner is the sole reason for keeping them looking and feeling so young. To some extent, I agree. It is contributors like fresh air and increased physical activity – both in and out of the bedroom – that are scientifically proven to preserve the ageing process –

all traits most commonly associated with the younger bracket of the population.

Within reason, age is and should just be a number. Trading your ex in for a younger model is somewhat of a trend – just look at some of the scandals and love rats throughout history and the lessons they've taught us. And I'm sure you've witnessed similar behaviour. If we are encouraging single folk to do as they so please, why is it ever only women branded with unsavoury names after displaying this particular behaviour? Think about it; when a woman gets a new partner she's either a cradle snatcher or a grave robber… and a man behaving in the same way gets to keep his 'stud status'. Why are we always the cougars and the gold-diggers and never on the receiving end of a pat on the back and a dirty laugh? It all boils down to age old sexism – and the best advice I could give anyone looking for a partner of any age? As long as your partner is age appropriate (legally allowed to be wining, dining and sixty-nining with you), and fully consensual, do what the fuck you want and prioritise what makes you happy.

I have no shame in admitting that I'm a high maintenance woman and, whilst toy boys and younger men might work for you, they most definitely don't for me. In an attempt to bag myself an experienced beau, I've wound up dabbling with friends of my father, too. I must stress here, this was not a village elder and choirgirl scandal. It was some pretty intense, explicit picture sharing, and a small age gap of 27 years. Regardless of how awkward it may have been for the other parties involved - and it really fucking was – if you're hot and single, you'd better believe I'm going to spark an interest. Irrespective of your age being more than double mine.

Enjoying a younger lover also ensures that you bear full witness to their egos. Confidence (in both ovaries and brovaries) is my favourite trait, but an over-inflated ego is not. And young men can't handle rejection. Trust me, honey, she didn't decline your number because she's 'probably a lesbian', she turned you down because you're off your face and have already asked three of her friends for theirs. And how many of your man-friends and such have complained of being 'friend-zoned'? BRB, I'm having an aneurism at the thought.

Chapter 9

The word 'slut' attacks women for their right to say yes and the phrase 'friend zone' attacks them for their right to say no.

There's no such thing as the friend zone. Yeah, I said it, and it's probably about time we stopped using it as an excuse for not getting what we want. Really, the 'friend zone' is a socially constructed coping mechanism used primarily by men to make us women feel guilty about rejecting them. It's essentially a cushion, used to soften the blow to the rejected party's ego (that bastard thing is always getting in the way).

As I believe it, the phrase was first coined in 1994 by yours and my favourite sitcom *Friends*. You remember - Joey dubbed Ross the "mayor of the friend zone". Whilst seemingly gender-neutral (yay), the 'friend zone' is undoubtedly sexist (soooo not yay). The phrase is programming society to believe that basic human decency entitles you to attention and affection from the recipient. It is allowing people to penalize those who reject their interest in them and takes a stand against the idea that we are all equal.

It's OK to like someone and not be attracted to them. I like Karen in the HR department at work but I don't want to rip her clothes off. It should never be apparent that a person – woman, man or non-binary - has to apologise for their naivety in thinking that they could keep platonic friends. Yes, I have been found 'guilty' of not being attracted to men who were attracted to me and really wanted me to return their feelings. As much as you may want to, you can't force yourself to feel attraction towards anyone. Regardless of how many other wonderful qualities your friend may have, without attraction, there is no relationship - and that's totally fine. I guess finding out you've been 'friend zoned' is a similar discovery to unveiling that someone you valued as a person and friend, really only wanted to get you into bed. Friendship is a relationship to be eternally grateful for, and yet we are portraying it as a punishment rather than a privilege.

Rejection is shite - I get it! It hurts when someone doesn't like you back. But no one owes you anything; no one is obligated to give you what you want. Sure, sex is a human need, but it is not something you have a right to and, again, will never be owed it. They either like you, or they don't. And that's life. That is what dating and being single is all about. When you tell someone how you feel and they yay or nay you, have your answer. An answer that should be accepted and respected.

I can't be the only one growing tired of 'nice guys'

complaining about being friend zoned by a woman. If you've abandoned your friendship with someone as a result of their wish to remain platonic, and proceed to complain that she friend zoned you because women are never interested in dating nice guys, then you just aren't a nice guy. Being a 'nice guy' doesn't entitle you to sex. Nothing does. Ever. If you didn't get what you wanted, learn from your mistakes and try again. Minus the shaming of innocent women, of course.

"Thinking you are owed something for not being an asshole, makes you an asshole." *- Desireé Dallagiacomo & Justin Lamb - "The Friend Zone"*

Society is using this ridiculous turn of phrase in an act of shaming. The word 'slut' attacks women for their right to say yes and the phrase 'friend zone' attacks them for their right to say no. The assumption that, once a person has indicated interest in a friend, said friend is obligated to reward the interest with a relationship or sex, completely eradicates a person's right to choose. This is what consent is all about, and it's actually terrifying that people still don't understand that. Everyone has the right to say "yes" or "no" to any sexual encounter. Everyone has the right to give, or not give, consent. Everyone has the right to have their decision respected. When a person's consent is violated, then that person has been sexually assaulted. So, please, let's stop using the friend zone as an excuse. They sought friendship, you sought more. Why not leave it at that instead of bad-mouthing their right to choose.

Chapter 10

*When women support each other,
incredible things happen.*

Yes, yes, I know. I'd be hypocritical to say that men are the root of all that is wrong in the world. I do anyway, though. But I shouldn't. We women can also be right fuckers, and often need to change our actions in the same way we call out men to change theirs.

I was a pretty god awful teen. Through my pent up sexual frustration and without a clue of how to release it, I shut myself off from the majority of my blood relatives. Still pissed that they ruined my life via the dissolving of my cherry popping plans, I adopted a hard exterior and, essentially, became a bitch. In one summer holiday, I had subconsciously transformed myself to the devil's daughter, with a demeanour that his worshippers would envy. I automatically assumed everyone was out to get me and in reaction learned how to bite back. And not a soft, puppy nibble, either.

Much in the way that I currently devour double cheeseburgers in four elegant mouthfuls, I could go from

0-100 in a matter of milliseconds. In that biting process, it wasn't unfamiliar for me to lash out, blame other people for my own issues and pick fault in almost everything and everyone I saw. I learned the hard way that there are few people you'll come across in life as small-minded, petty and frightfully bitchy as nasty girls with more issues than Vogue. Girl hate was so prominent back then and I should know, I was one of the nastiest and bitchiest of them all.

I didn't have a lightbulb moment. There was no one day that I woke up and suddenly decided to stop being such a heinous cowbag. What actually happened was totally natural; time. I started to live less selfishly, open my eyes and actually look at the world around me. What I discovered? Not so nice. It is the 21st century and every night when I tirelessly scroll through social media before bed, I am still met with an abundance of comments from keyboard warriors insulting and putting each other down.

It has almost become culture for women and girls to automatically pick fault with one another. And why? Most of, if not all of us, have insecurities. There are aspects of our personalities, lives and bodies we wish we could alter and can't. That is normal, and we can and should learn to accept that, right? So why is it that, when in defence, our first strike normally aims straight for the personal - picking specific insults that we know are going to hurt our opponent? No one out there is better than you, they are just different, and learning to accept each other's differences is seriously overdue.

Who are we to determine 'perfection'? I'll give you a

clue, there's no such thing. Beauty isn't skin deep and it isn't something you achieve by looking a certain way. It is something you are born with and should be taught to embrace because it's completely unique amongst beings. I promise you, it's not defined by how clear your skin is, how hysterical your jokes are or whether or not you've got that sarong that all the Kardashians are wearing. Currently, there are certain stigmas hanging around the word 'society'. And rightly so. It is trying to teach us to be a certain way, to admire and yearn to be someone else; rather than accepting and loving ourselves. By singling out someone else's flaws, we are pushing that person to feel like they aren't good enough, and like they should want to be someone else. We should be encouraging the women of today; young, old, big, little - it doesn't matter - to embrace their beautiful souls, to do what they damn well please (as long as they aren't hurting themselves or others) and to spread nothing but love.

I have a theory. For centuries, women have been tirelessly and mercilessly digging each other out. Consider the fact that after playing audience to it for so many years, perhaps nearby men then deemed it acceptable to discriminate and criticize women because those who are meant to be our 'sisters' and support team started doing it first? So I quit, cold turkey. I stopped judging other people on the way they looked, the way they dressed and the way they were. I stopped blaming every other person on this planet other than myself for mistakes and issues I needed to tackle and I started noticing all of the wonderful qualities people had. To be optimistic enough to always see the good in something is a gift. Let's now all make a promise to only see the good in people. Trust me, this is how I'm learning to love myself. I rid my life of all the nastiness and negativity and began paving my own path to happiness.

It is empowering to empower another person. Aside from (maybe) an orgasm, there is no feeling more satisfying. When women support each other, incredible things happen. And, as women, we are fighting a pretty tough battle; against history, against sexism, against racism, against homophobia, against the patriarchy and against ourselves. We NEED the support! We NEED to work together as one giant, unstoppable force to be reckoned with.

It's high time that we women got to grips with the idea that our lives don't revolve around anyone else. You weren't put on this earth to be a bit of eye candy or a pretty little stay at home spouse. I mean, if you really think about it on a chicken and egg scale, the ready-to-be-fertilised-egg never chases the sperm. So why should a woman ever chase a man?! Your career will never up and leave in the middle of the night because it decided not to love you anymore.

"Sweetheart, marry your goals. Remain committed to success. Be loyal to your dreams, it's okay to choose yourself." – *R.H. Sin*

And, it is. I am a firm believer that the most important lesson that a woman could ever learn is to be selfish. Put yourself first. Always. There is no other situation I can comprehend in which you will thrive by pushing people in front of you. I'm obviously not telling you to sabotage your competitors and sleep with married men – you need the sisterhood more than you think – but you do you. Don't let boys or girls or diets or society stand in the way of anything you desire. There is no force more powerful than a woman determined to rise. Empowering other women should always be at the top of your 'to do' list – even prior to masturbation. Make like the drunk girl in the bathroom, and tell your girlfriends, sisters and colleagues how much you love their shoes, how great they are and how bomb they look that day.

WOMAN UP

Chapter 11

We should be using our greatest tools to spread the word and grow our International Girl Gang.

Make no mistake, empowerment doesn't mean loving every other woman alive. Eliminating girl hate by no small stretch means you have to get along with every other woman. It just means you refrain from tearing them down or discriminating against them for their sex. It's letting go of internalized misogyny, envy and jealousy. It means not undermining the sisterhood with gender-based insults and not pushing each other under the bus for men. It's putting a stop to holding other women to the arbitrary and restrictive gender roles that we've been socialized into.

"No one can make you feel inferior without your consent." – *Eleanor Roosevelt*

We should be using our greatest tools to spread the word and grow our International Girl Gang. Through mediums such as social media, we have already

nd. The Time's Up movement has
storm, and, at long last, women
rward and taking a stand against
e industry and what really goes on
r too long these truths have been
h victims and supporters coming
forward, causing a stir and calling out unequal pay and sexual assault and harassment in the workplace. #MeToo, the trending campaign that brought uproar on various social sites, is giving women a platform to speak their truth. Women who, for far too long, have been silenced, shamed and discouraged from sharing their stories.

These campaigns are ground-breaking and important, not only because they are exposing abusers, but because of the millions of people watching, listening and relating worldwide. As a sexual assault survivor, I can't stress enough what it means to have what seems like a world of women standing behind you, and those in the limelight fighting your cause. So, what does this tell us? We need to keep talking. We need to raise our voices and our concerns until we are unapologetically loud. We need to empower ourselves and each other and make public knowledge of the issues that women everywhere are facing. We don't need to find our voice - we already have a voice, we just need to learn how to use it.

2018 marked 100 years of suffrage. A century since the first countries granted women a political vote. An incredible milestone, but, looking at the bigger picture – just how far have we come? Women in the UK weren't included in the Equal Pay Act until 1970 – and this still hasn't abolished the gender pay gap. In recent months, the BBC shone a somewhat unflattering light and published the earnings of their highest paid media stars. As of April 2019, organisations with more than 250 employees were required to publish the gender pay gap for their company, quarterly. Whilst this is undoubtedly a step in the right direction, it will inevitably act as evidence that, despite having the same judicial rights on paper as our male counterparts, we are a long way off being equal.

I'm really trying to pave a way for this sex positivity thing, and it becomes increasingly harder to do following the influence and behaviour from the certain wank puffins disguising as our political leaders. The USA is currently being run by a serial sex pest billionaire with a history of irrefutable sexism, racism, discrimination and assault crimes. We aren't going to get anywhere if we're still objectifying women in front of the entire world. No thanks, Don. American women are living in fear for their sexual health and desperately clinging on to the rights to their own body. 2017 revealed that a case of female genital mutilation is either discovered or treated at a medical appointment in England every hour. Two hundred million women around the world are currently suffering the effects of FGM.

We live in a world where period poverty is real life.

Where people cannot afford sanitary protection, and women are taxed on said products as 'luxuries'. Research by Women For Independence recently found that one in five Scottish women have struggled to buy tampons or pads, instead having to use toilet paper, rags, old clothes, and even newspapers. Glossy magazines and less reliable newspapers still make their money from dehumanizing women. Pitting them against each other and pulling out and publicly shaming their 'flaws', feeding into diet culture and the lack of self confidence in our younger generations - portraying everything that is wrong with the media. Learn to respect and thank the women around you; be it your mother, sister, best friend, co-worker or even she who serves you in your local supermarket. Thank them for doing their bit, and then do your bit. Pledge your support to the cause, call out gender-based bias and challenge convention. Let it be known that we stand together in solidarity, pushing for what we deserve.

Just try and be kind. I'm not telling you to smile at strangers and strike up a pen pal relationship with prison-inhabiting murderers, but saying thank you and offering out your Marlboro lights, even though you've only got four left, will never go amiss. People are dealing with varying amounts of shit at all times. Just because they don't chat openly about it whilst waiting for the bus to town, doesn't mean it isn't happening. Look at what's happening politically around the world – that is very real and very, very serious, and we seldom bother to discuss that over our morning coffees. Also, generationally, we should probably start being nicer to old people, otherwise they'll continue to think that all youth are thug-like. Considering how polite we Brits are meant to be, some of us are real twats. No amount of perfect queuing and giving up your tube seat to someone eight months pregnant will excuse the behaviour of racist, sexist, Britain First loving sociopaths that think it's ok to shame someone for their culture, background, sex, religion or choices. Fuck off, the lot of you.

Whilst we're on the subject of being a little nicer, let's make a vow to stop tearing women down for being successful. Having seen it first hand through the working mothers and single CEOs that I've associated with, it's been nigh on impossible to ignore the scrutiny that they face. These women are not intimating - you are intimidated.

WOMAN UP

Chapter 12

If I had a penny for every time I've been described as 'intimidating', I'd finally be able to buy myself a decent replica of Lady Gaga's meat dress, but made entirely of Wagyu beef and hand-reared veal.

If I had a penny for every time I've been described as 'intimidating', I'd finally be able to buy myself a decent replica of Lady Gaga's meat dress, but made entirely of Wagyu beef and hand-reared veal. I am loud, definitely a little annoying, and I'm very, very open. Seriously, I'm not afraid to spill the beans on my sexual history whilst waiting in Boots for the morning after pill, an audience of 16 strangers queueing behind me. My sexpertise and resulting confidence has made me the most loud and proud person I know. I'm not afraid to voice whatever I'm thinking, but can't help but notice the often negative response. As an outgoing and confident person, I've had qualities that I should be (and I am) proud of, pin pointed as reasons as to why I was single and am unpopular. I'm sure it was solely down to this, and nothing to do with the fact that I have a permanent resting bitch face and a particular fondness for aggressive feminist slogan t-shirts. Does confidence and success really scare people off? Why are women always told not to come off 'too strong'? At risk of emasculating men? I call bullshit. Pop culture encourages women to bat their eyelashes and wear passive lip gloss instead of bold lipstick to draw in a suitor. Bill Clinton cheated on (the highly successful) Hillary with Monica, an intern. Mr Big married Natasha over Carrie in order to feel like more of a man.

Independence is an attractive trait in both sexes, but how is this defined being a woman? What exactly is being independent? Fending for yourself? Remembering to switch on the dishwasher and separate your colours from your whites? Is that independence? Changing your own light bulbs? Mowing your own lawn? Executing all the chores that typically a man would see to? I am one for shouting from the rooftops about women categorically not needing men - and I'm pretty damn certain they don't. Minus cooking my steak to bloody perfection and the occasional pest control, I can absolutely take care of myself. And sweet baby Jesus knows that should I stumble across an activity that I struggle to face; I can lie back and thank him for amazing friends and great dildos. So why should a woman's self-proclaimed independence repel men?

If successful and confident women really do intimidate guys, then it's through no fault of our own. We are products of our environment. It just so happens our contemporary surroundings are the result of a feminist revolution that's developed in all aspects of our lives. In short - we've gradually been persuaded that as a group, we do not need men. And believe me, not all of that persuasion has come from me running around my home town in my t-shirt of the day, actively boosting the drive of every woman I meet to do as she pleases. We need men to fertilize our eggs and change the TV channel when we're too lazy to lift an arm, but at the end of the day – men will never be a necessity.

"A man is not a necessity, a man is a luxury. Like a dessert." - *Cher*

It's the 21st Century and women have come a long way. We're beginning to surpass men in many areas. We have more masters and college degrees, better grades in general and, with any luck, it is estimated that by 2025, more than half the primary breadwinners in America will be women. There will forever be men, regardless of how much time has passed, who hold up the male chauvinism glory days of the 1950s as the golden social model. A successful woman knows her worth. She knows what she deserves and knows she shouldn't have to settle for second best. We are smart enough to have picked up on the fact that men tend to favour less accomplished, 'easier' women, and in turn, we have begun to use independence as a self-defence mechanism to avoid getting hurt or betrayed. I've always known what I wanted from a man (humour, thick thighs and great sex) and have never been afraid to chase after it. And when I say chase, I mean sprint. As fast as I can, towards the nearest rugby pitch. A clever girl (with an ass that won't quit) who knows what she's looking for? What exactly is unattractive about that sentence?! She (I) sounds GREAT! But, again, maybe that's from a woman's perspective.

Maybe men fear that successful women wouldn't be able to balance their time between personal and business matters. Well, let me assure you that this is not the case. The majority of working women I know juggle their successful careers, maintain relationships and sustain their chosen lifestyles, including fabulous social lives. To conclude - if what you have, or are capable of doing, scares a man off, how is it by any small measure fair for a man to deem your unfaltering drive as anything less than a celebration? Don't ever apologise for your successes or confidence. Don't settle for anything less than what you think you deserve. It's better and healthier to be alone than to be in an inadequate relationship.

I discovered my true confidence in my late teens. I started to notice and learn to accept compliments, and the fact that people were laughing at my jokes. It was a turning point for both my social and professional careers. And, with this newfound confidence, came a whole lot of sass. I've always been a bit of a sassy diva, but this was like the homecoming after years of having my self-worth and confidence beaten down by society's mallet. As a toddler I was known to scold my parents for dressing me incorrectly and I had no issue in informing them when they were boring me. Oh, and I tried to convince them to change my name to Jasmine. Like the Princess and Disney's epitome of an independent woman, note. Despite my very best efforts to come off as more exotic, no amount of writing this on my school work books and refusing to answer to anything else changed their mind.

My newly renewed confidence presented itself in a number of ways. I was nearly always grounded (a result of all the drugs, house parties and scandalous pictures) and so snuck out. A lot. I would join my family for Friday evening dinner, make up an excuse about buying cigarettes or dropping a top to a friend, and then stay out until I saw fit. Normally, to avoid awkward encounters with my father that same evening, I would find an excuse to shack up with someone hot and local. Worked a treat every time. It didn't, however, cool his temper when I eventually showed up back at home, 14 hours later and in the same clothes and make up as the night before. Sorry, Dad.

If I wanted to talk to a boy, I no longer fluttered around, asking my friends to ask his friends if he thought I was a bit of alright. I didn't spend hours pouring over his Bebo page to then see him in person and avoid all eye contact. I told them. I marched up to them in the common room and made it very clear that I was interested, and they would be foolish not to be.

I don't know how I can honestly remember this,

considering the quantity of Lambrini that I had inhaled prior, but I went to a fancy dress birthday party once, dressed as 'PC Pleasure'. This was the sluttiest outfit I could get my hands on and the buttons that ran the full length of the dress, which wasn't all that long in the first place, had a habit of popping open to reveal my then-bald private parts whenever I moved my legs. Don't get me wrong, I looked great, and if I could fit more than a wrist into the outfit now, I'm sure I would recycle it for other events. Whilst looking like a red light resident was highly desirable at the time, the outfit was really purchased and paraded to catch the attention of my latest crush. Unfortunately, it wasn't only his attention that I caught, and mere hours into the 18th soiree, I was swiftly removed from the cubicle of the men's toilet that we were fumbling in, and the venue entirely. By this point, I had lost track of all of my friends and was in dire need of some chicken nuggets and my bed. My next hurdle was trying to get back to my friend's house, without the phone or purse that I had left in her bag. I did what anyone in the same situation would do; and flopped one of my tits out as attempted payment for my cab ride. He refused to drive me home, and instead offered me a cash alternative of £1.86, so must have been really busy or something…

My skills of persuasion have grown with me as a person. I've absolutely nailed going to a bar with no money, and returning home suitably pissed. And yeah, I'm still a feminist if other men are buying me drinks. I am independent. I am strong. Rich? I am not. Make no mistake, for approximately four days post pay day, I am happy to share the love and can often be found propping up the bar, paying for everyone to have a voddy and a good time. But there lies the problem. I am such a wannabe baller just after I get paid, that I end up living like a pauper for the other 21 days of the month. And, believing in gender equality, I purchase drinks for both my male and female peers. So if I have been invited out and it's dangerously close to pay day, you'd better believe I'm going to accept the kind offer of a free double gin.

WOMAN UP

Chapter 13

I'm a feminist, regardless of whether I engage in sex, think about sex and write about sex.

I'm a feminist. Join me, it's great. I love women and men and people who don't identify as whatever they wish, as well as people of every race, religion and sexual orientation. I want us all to have complete equality. Like, that's it. That's feminism. And no, we shouldn't have to change the name to anything other than 'common sense'. Arguing that your refusal of feminism is based on its feminine name and branding is irrelevant when we're all part of MANkind. Mic drop.

"Feminism is not a dirty word. It does not mean you hate men, it does not mean you hate girls that have nice legs and a tan, and it does not mean you are a 'bitch' or 'dyke'; it means you believe in equality." – Kate Nash

It's the 21st century, and women everywhere are still being discriminated against and not treated like equals.

A century after the suffragettes fought for our right to vote and still women are behind men in too many ways. It's tiring to constantly hear and read that women continue to be treated as objects and subjects less deserving than men. All over the planet, in first, second and third world countries, women still don't have equal status to men - neither legally nor socially. Whilst there's no justification for this, it has been happening since the dawn of time and shows no immediate plan to halt. Women are fighting for their rights every single day – and this is why we need feminism. Contrary to ridiculous but popular belief, feminism isn't the act of hating a man. It isn't a group of women clubbing together to burn their bras and boycott blowjobs – it is human beings standing for equality between the sexes.

Thanks to Kimberle Crenshaw and her 1989 revelation, I identify as an Intersectional Feminist. In simpler terms, certain groups of women have a variety of facets in life that they have to deal with. Feminism will never be one-size-fits-all. Until the mainstream feminist movement starts listening to all of the various groups of women within it, then it will continue to stand still without hope of moving forward. While this concept has been around longer than I have, only recently has it been brought to light and thrown into feminist debate.

You wouldn't believe me if I told you the amount of hate messages and mail I receive shaming me as a feminist and telling me I couldn't possibly believe in woman's rights. Apparently, because I am not only sexually active, but also a slut, I've subconsciously given up my right to be a feminist. Who'd have thought! Engaging in something personally enjoyable has left me unable to stand up for women, who are all doing exactly the same thing! Give me a fecking break. If anything, this has only enhanced my right to call myself a feminist. I've been on the receiving end of a harsh tongue and I've been shamed for most of my young adult life. Even before I lost my virginity, people had branded me with derogatory names. Slut shaming is a huge problem in the 21st century, and it's baffling how many men (and a shit tonne of women) think it's acceptable to call others out on their private decisions. Each and every person on this earth should have the right to do what (and who) they please without being criticized for their actions or behaviour.

I'm a feminist, regardless of whether I engage in sex, think about sex and write about sex - as I do most days of my life. I've been anonymously told, through both my blog and social channels, that I couldn't be a feminist because I was part of the problem. Apparently, writing about sex forbids me from wanting equality, and the two can't just go hand in hand. Enlighten me, then, as to why it's generally accepted for a man to talk about sex and openly discuss his sexual conquests yet when I, a woman, do so - it's regarded as slutty, uncouth and unacceptable.

So does it mean I'm not a real feminist because I

make my boyfriend breakfast on the occasion, clean up after us and host dinner parties in a 1950's housewife style? No, does it fuck. Gender Essentialism (the assumption that women and men and inherently different and should be treated accordingly by society) is not feminist. What makes a girl, a girl? Is it an apron? A brood of well-behaved children? An immaculate home? And what makes a man? A wife? It sure as hell isn't a vagina. Some days I wake up and want to stay at home, waiting for my boyfriend's return from work and baking bitesize delicious pies in between hoovering and dusting the home, and some days I wake up and have the urge to jump on a plane to the USA and chain myself to the front door of Planned Parenthoods and clinics alike to contribute my fight to their needy battle. By making my boyfriend a sandwich or doing something he's asked me to do, I'm not conforming to the housewife stereotypical standard and I'm absolutely not any less of a feminist.

Ostensibly, I'm not a real feminist because I shave my legs, care for my appearance and wear make-up. Do you think it's ever occurred to people that women don't dress for men? I do not shave my legs, expertly draw on my eyebrows and brush my hair *most* mornings to submit to the aesthetic standards of the male gaze. I spend my mornings preening myself for me, and that's all. I am the most confident woman I know, and making myself feel glamorous and highlighting my assets enhances that confidence - something I think that all women need to learn to do. And there's no greater feeling than getting into a freshly made bed with newly-bald legs and sliding around like a carefree dolphin. Hours of entertainment, I shit you not.

Ask my boyfriend – he has hinted multiple times that I book myself in for a Hollywood wax and my reaction is the same time and time again; no. Because I simply don't want to. I'd rather look down at my nether region and be reminded that I am a powerful fucking woman. Plus, I'm growing quite fond of how fluffy, soft and comforting it is. If anything, my deciding where and when I wish to shave is a feminist act within itself, as I'm choosing to do what makes me comfortable and I am not letting anyone else make decisions regarding my body for me. I am exercising my right to choose and standing by what I want.

I can't be a feminist because I post nearly-nude selfies on Instagram, right? Or share them with my friends, family and strangers from the pub? Because, who even knows what would happen if everyone suddenly decided to be comfortable with their bodies and confident enough to show them off. A huge industry would go out of business, for starters. All in all, it's probably about time we stopped categorising feminism and accepted all things Intersectional - don't you think?

I am a feminist because I believe in complete gender equality. Women should, like men, be able to live their lives as they see fit. For me, the world needs feminism so our gender no longer can act as a burden or obstacle to what we want and need. I want my daughters to have the same rights as my sons. We women should be able to do the same job as a man, with the same pay cheque. Similarly, men should be entitled to be a stay-at-home father/husband should they so desire. Traditional gender roles just don't work for everyone. I am a feminist because women are repetitively sexualised and objectified - magazine covers? Women are scrutinised for their weight, asked about their relationships or shown posing semi-nude while men are credited for their skills and professions. This has become such norm now, that breastfeeding in public has been ruled by some as disgusting and un-necessary; inevitably all down to the over-sexualisation of women. I am a feminist because 1 in 5 women between the ages of 16 and 59 have experienced some kind of sexual violence, and 97% of rapists will never spend a single day in prison. There are still countries in this world who punish women after they have been sexually assaulted. I am a feminist because I believe that women can wear what they want without being an invitation or an excuse and sleep with who they want without being called a slut. I am a feminist because 'like a girl' remains to be used as an insult. I am a feminist because we need to stop telling our daughters that that little boy hit, kicked or hurt her because 'he likes her'. I am a feminist because sexist jokes stopped being funny a long, long time ago. I am a feminist because around 3 million girls still fall victim to Female Genital Mutilation every year. Above all, I am a feminist because I still have to explain why I am a feminist.

We really need to start empowering one another - it's a long time coming. I can tell you from years of valuable experience that the only way women can win is to stop tearing each other down and start building each other up. Strong women would struggle to be as strong without the support of their sisters. Our culture pits women against each other - we aren't programmed to be sugar, spice and all things nice to all other women, but we need to be. You've all seen Mean Girls, I'm sure; so why hasn't everyone taken Ms Norbury's statement "You all have got to stop calling each other sluts and whores. It just makes it OK for guys to call you sluts and whores" on board? This 'girl world' isn't scary - we just need to eliminate the feelings of hatred, jealousy and bitchiness towards our fellow females that are polluting our chance to group together. It should not be foolish for me to imagine that there will ever be a time, in the near future at least, where all women love and appreciate one another like they should. Someone will always push against the grain and hate. Regardless of the exceptions, we need to start working as one in order to obtain the equality we all deserve.

WOMAN UP

Chapter 14

Anything that compromises your happiness should be CTRL, ALT, DELETED from your life.

Alas, the latest flaw I've noticed in our arguably misogynistic society is who should say 'I Love You' first. If you haven't already clocked, in my relationship; it was me. Technically, I initially said it on the first date. But that was a mistake, and a direct result of hysterical laughter and, therefore, a severe lack of oxygen to the brain. I suspect he was as mortified as I was, but hid it very well. Around eight weeks later, I told him again – and this time, I meant it. Or, I thought I did anyway. In hindsight – I may have been somewhat overexcited at my first proper boyfriend who wanted to call himself my boyfriend, and jumped the gun a little. Make no mistake, I was definitely falling for him, but I didn't come to a realisation of just how strong my feelings were until we were together around six months, and he left the country for a week.

As sweet as this anecdote is, it's not the point. I put myself out there first. I get it – a proclamation of love is a pretty big deal. To even BE in love is nothing short of spectacular. I, personally, believe that love as a whole, earns itself a substandard reputation and is portrayed as an emotion for the weak. Love IS everything it's cracked up to be, and that is why people are so cynical about it. It's worth fighting for, being brave for and risking everything for. If we are honest with ourselves, I think both men and women hold off on dropping the L bomb, even when they know it's the truth. Are we afraid of rejection? Undeniably. Think of the stories you've read and the tales you've heard. Of lovers denying their other halves sex, and even strangers declining the offer of a date. Their fate inevitably coming to a harrowing end. Murder, physical violence, sexual assault, kidnap – all because some self-righteous bastard couldn't handle being rejected. Unsurprisingly, in their true stereotypical self-entitled style - most of the perpetrators in such situations are men.

The argument that women can't be the first to say those three little words almost mirrors the idea that most have ingrained, of men having to always make the first move. Whilst there is no excuse for patriarchal behaviour, this is generally generational and an idea handed down from parents and grandparents alike. Millennials – wake up and smell the avocado toast! We should not be contributing to any ideals or aspects of a sexist society. If you fancy someone, ask them out – regardless of their (or your) sex. This should be no different to saying I Love You for the first time.

Don't be afraid to put yourself out there. Go forth, and conquer! Live on the edge! Pee into the wind! But, seriously, why the fear? If they reject your proclamation it will simply be because A. they are not quite there yet, which is totally forgivable, everyone is different. Or, B. Because they are an asshole and need to be sacked off imminently.

As an independent woman, I rely on men for almost nothing. I look after myself and love myself and, as a result, am in charge and control of my own feelings. Therefore, it should be my decision as and when I share them. When I tell people that I said 'I Love You' first, the majority answer 'because you're a feminist'? To which my answer is always the same – no, not because I am a feminist, but because I am a woman who (like all other women should) does what she damn well pleases. My advice to any and all people in relationships (and whether they ask for it or not), is that there is no greater tool than honesty.

So, yeah, I told him I loved him on the first date. And I drank too much champagne and burped into his mouth mid-snog. And I let him put it in my butt. And look at me now – in a stable and happy relationship, despite behaving in an 'unladylike' way and being a complete hoe while breaking the 'don't you dare fuck on the first date if you ever want to find happiness ever' rule.

He has changed me as a person. I'm less of a bitch, and my patience has grown to that of a saint having to share my home and life with another person. Is it a universal trait for men to use every single available pot, pan and utensil whilst cooking a meal? Literally, the boy makes toast and all of a sudden the dishwasher is boasting spatulas, a wok and a broken sieve. And do all athletes leave their wet and dirty kit on the floor directly in front of the front door for a minimum of 3-5 working days? He has his flaws (as do the rest of us), but all in all, he's a pretty fantastic human being and great at occasionally having sex with me after I've nagged him for an hour.

I am lucky in having a wonderful support system. Whilst I am a pretty damn (and self-certified) strong and resilient bad bitch, everyone needs a little support every once in a while. Thanks to the big D back in 2k12 (I mean divorce, although I'm certain there were a few more big Ds that year…), I now have a whole host of siblings. Two full sibs and five halves. And, yes, Christmas is really fucking expensive. I know I'm biased, but they are all completely amazing, albeit at the very top of the painfully irritating spectrum, as younger siblings are, and have made an excellent addition to a family that I'd deemed as almost perfect.

This won't come as much as a surprise, but your parents probably do know best after all. Damn. They've made the mistakes you've made, and have been in your shitty and sticky situations. And then went on to live for another fair few decades, and move on with their lives. So you may as well listen to what they've got to say to you - even if you don't like it and you pretend that you've got your headphones in and can't hear. Your mum and dad have your best interests at heart – despite how fucking naggy and annoying they may be. Mine are saints for putting up with the shit I've dragged them through over the last quarter of a Century. Good on ya, Ma and Pa! Also, tell them you love them once in a while. It won't hurt, and they'll like hearing it.

I grew up close with my cousins. Honestly, I am baffled when friends speak of cousins that they seldom keep in contact with or have never even ever met. My cousins are the reason that I saw a vagina for the very first time (it was hers, and she was three and had only just discovered it). We grew up like sisters. And so, not only do I have seven 'official' siblings, but five further scuzzens – the imaginative word for any and all sister cousins, just like us. We, alongside my various aunties and uncles, are a family unit and you don't want to mess with us. Think The Mitchells from EastEnders, but with a whole lot more hair and a wealth of sass. It's really nice to be able to say that I am happiest when with my family, drinking red wine until 4am in the morning and singing at the top of our lungs to literally anything we can remember the words to (but more often than not, Stevie Wonder).

You've gotta have people to support you. You've just gotta! Without them, I would be screwed. Equally, my most favourite life lesson and what I really hope I remember for my next time around, is the importance of ridding yourself of toxicity. I'm talking relationships, people and situations. Anything that compromises your happiness should be CTRL, ALT, DELETED from your life. We don't know what happens after death. No one has yet come back to tell us about their journey into the fiery depths, or what it was like to live as a tortoise. So, until there is full and concrete evidence that you might get to give it another shot, I'm fairly convinced that this is your only chance. Live every day as if it were your last. Because what if there is an afterlife, and it's sat in a medium to comfortable chair, watching your life story on repeat. You'd be mortified and really bloody bored if your show reel was you repeatedly taking that nasty ex back, or living any way other than happy.

The kind of toxic people I'm referring to here is anyone who isn't supportive, love-showing, positive, important, or appear to be conflict magnets. There is no shame in cutting people loose. And it's OK if those people are your best friends, in-laws, spouses or family members. You always come first, and there should be no room in your divine life for anyone who isn't understanding of what you want and need. Surrounding yourself with only positive vibes and energy will change your whole outlook.

My significant other is just that, the most significant being in my life. Sure, dear old mum and dad are pretty fucking awesome, and always keen to help me out when I need it, but this is an entirely different relationship. We live together, making it very hard for me to hide my feelings. And you'll soon get to know me and my reluctancy to only talk about how I actually feel when I am absolutely hooned…

So whilst my family and friends are amazing once I reach out to them – my beau is there for it all. For the laughter, the anger and the crying over a pot of burnt pasta.

I knew he was different from the moment I first met him during 2015's Rugby World Cup, at our local club. I had been previously warned by a mutual friend that he was new to the area and most likely in need of a friend. Particularly a friend with a blow dry like mine and a juicy double. So, I introduced myself. We hit it off instantly, and by the time we had shared numerous smoke breaks and an accidental flash of my best tit, he told me that I was his 'ideal woman'. Admittedly, he was in the process of concluding his current relationship but, like the good girl I am, I waited until he had officially ended it and was on the market and ripe for the picking. We went pretty deep, pretty damn fast. Before our first date, he had already told me that he was worried about me sleeping with other people. So I didn't. Which, believe me, is an incredible testament to my being, and a true expression of how much I love him.

WOMAN UP

Chapter 15

I suffered at the hands of petty, bitchy 18 year olds until the day I left school.

I took my own virginity. I was 15 and the perpetrator (or... penetrator?) was a carrot I had stolen from my mother's vegetable drawer. I was still trapped in co-ed hell, and scathingly wanted to have something to tell my friends. I had no access to real life penis, so this happened to be the next best thing. Despite the fury I still held over my parents, I opted not to return the carrot after use. It was a decision that I didn't take lightly, but one I had pondered on for approximately twelve months prior which, in hindsight, seems ridiculous considering it was literally an inanimate object. It hurt, and didn't last for much longer than half a minute. After that I gave up on the idea of being sexually active, albeit with a common vegetable, and focused on my studies. And, by focussing on my studies, I mean getting drunk alone in my bedroom with an ancient bottle of apple flavoured liquor and being 'formally asked to leave' that all-girls school I was attending, following my sunbathing stint on the main lawn. The focus on anything other than sex lasted approximately four days.

In the coming months I ditched my legume love and graduated onto the likes of hairbrush handles, body spray bottles and, eventually, the sacred electric toothbrush – the one instrument that managed to maintain a permanent position in my bedside drawer. Just a reminder, masturbation is a completely normal, human act. If only I had been able to string said sentence together after my poor, now-grey mother walked in on me doubled over on her bathroom floor, experimenting with a travel sized bottle of Herbal Essences.

Alas, my little orange friend stood me in good stead. Losing my virginity was easy. I tweeted a running commentary of how the evening went and, afterwards, sent all of my closest friends the link to The Lonely Island's 'I Just Had Sex' to ensure there was no ambiguity in the matter.

It became apparent that my initial bout of fornication was so pain free and easy because he wasn't much of a snake charmer and hadn't quite mastered the art of anything other than completely un-rhythmic thrashing. So when round two with lover number two came around, I was convinced for days afterwards that he had punctured one of my lungs. It's an awful disappointment when someone so well-endowed has a severely inadequate personality – almost as if God had pumped the whole sum of his charisma allowance into one particular limb (and yes, it was like a tiny arm, so limb is appropriate).

He was 25, and I was almost 17. It was exciting, and his spoiling me with kind words and cheap perfume convinced me that this was it, and he surely loved me. Spoiler alert – he didn't. It did transpire, however, that he was quite worryingly peculiar and ended up asking me about our future children as I lay naked in the backseat of his Volvo following our first bout of coitus. First and last, I might add. It was only after our brief albeit intense affair that I found out he owed both his ex-girlfriend and family members a whopping sum of money. He has continued to pop back into my life from time to time ever since. His constant checking up on me until this point has been less caring and more creepy. When asked if I were seeing anyone at any given time, the answer 'no' would evoke the reaction "no one will ever want you" and 'yes' brought the chorus "you're a massive slag". Thanks, hun.

Regardless of that bout of excitement and how grown up I felt at the time, he was absolutely grooming me. I was 16-years-old, and he was nearly a decade my senior. Our first communication (after he'd added me as a friend on Facebook) was before my sixteenth birthday, meaning I was a child and he was a predator. Not to be confused with my ranting about cougars and my own affiliation with older men, as I am all for an age gap. But an age gap where everyone involved has been around the sun an appropriate amount of time, and not when any party is in the midst or on the cusp of childhood.

It all gets a bit misty from then on. My long term memory usually serves me very well unless, of course, I am trying to recall my lovers. I've even tried writing them down, but there's always between 10 - 20 that get accidentally missed off. My third intimate partner is seldom worth mentioning. Although he did re-appear around number 15 and tried a LOT harder. I had fancied him for a considerable few years and briefly dated him numerous times between my 16th and 18th birthdays. I have no hard feelings towards saying this, as I was witness to his improvement with age and technique, but my third sexual partner was my first bout of bad sex. The waterbed setting didn't help much either, mind. Romantic in theory, but really fucking difficult to manoeuvre. And a damn shame considering how long I'd spent pining for him. Let this be a lesson to all – it's best not to pick your future boyfriend based on how blue his eyes are.

The reason behind me re-inviting him to play the mating game was my desperation to not increase my numbers. I could say this was sad, really, considering I already knew we weren't sexually compatible, but I was a novice, and didn't truly know what sexual compatibility was. I knew we hadn't had great sex, because I remember thinking about what earrings best paired with the jumpsuit I had bought for a friend's 18th whilst he moaned into my hair.

Sweet dreams are made of reminiscing about years gone by, re-living nights out and past shags. If I'm ever sat at my desk with a glazed look in my eyes, know that I am re-living the years gone by. I used to parade out into our local market town on Friday, and nearest club location on a Saturday with a couple of girlfriends in particular. We would dress ourselves up to the tens (much like the nines, but with an extra layer of fake tan and eyelashes) and head out on the pull, week in, week out. Haters will say it sounds boring; but those were the best years of my growing up. I remember the excitement of pre-drinking, dancing around the living room and pre-packing my clutch bag for the evening; jammed with clean knickers, a toothbrush (both on the hopeful assumption that I wouldn't return home that evening) and a packet of mini cheddars. You know, in case I needed a pick me up or a pre-Maccies snack.

So, I'm a slut. Or so I've been told for the vast majority of my life. Sure, a lot of times it came from the mouths of men, but the majority of my insult hurlers have been female. The slur has become so commonly used that nowadays to receive it, the alleged incident doesn't even have to relate to sex. I suffered cruel mistreatment during my last year at school and all that those against me could muster up was 'slut'.

Like so many of us, my memories of my High School years are not my most pleasant. Kids are fucking cruel, and 16-18 year olds are much, much worse. Sure, I had tendencies to be a bit of a cow at times, but no rumours I passed on or ex-boyfriends I flirted with were worth the consequences I was subjected to. My final year, especially, was made hell by the majority of my yearbook who essentially based their entertainment around my misery, slut-shamed and belittled me and made me feel so fucking worthless, until I reached a pretty dark point.

Mean texts I could and can handle, but the public shaming on social media was a little harder to adjust to. I was tweeted about daily, and even compared to the first slice of bread in a loaf, as 'everybody touched me, but nobody wanted me'. Imaginative, but pretty brutal, huh? It was one of those times when your mum assures you that your mates are only acting out because they're jealous. You're never going to believe her saying that in the first instance, are you? Firstly because she's your mum and oh my gawwwddd what does SHE know about this heavy 17 year old turmoil?! And also because you're almost 18. You constantly feel like you're not good enough and why on earth would anyone be jealous of you? Anyway, looking back now, almost seven years later, and she just might have been right.

On a couple of occasions, I was told that I would be better off killing myself. I understand anger, frustration and what it's like to be really pissed at someone. But no amount of teenage girl dramatics excuses telling someone to consider suicide. It was horrifying and gives me chills even thinking about it. Had I not been as strong as I was or been without any support system at all, I wonder how I would have reacted. It almost doesn't bear thinking about.

The fall out, as they often do in high school, escalated to the point where I was left pretty much friendless. All but one member of our year group had turned against me, and happily joined the parade with metaphorical pitch forks and torches. The remaining memories of my last year in school are painful and involve being publicly humiliated, laughed at, and having rubbish thrown at me from all corners of the common room. So, yeah, pretty biblical shaming for little to no reason. In total, vicious honesty, I suffered at the hands of petty, bitchy 18-year-olds until the day I left school. Thankfully, I am a firm believer in everything happening for a reason, regardless of how hard it was to see at the time. What doesn't kill you actually does make you stronger, even if it takes you the best part of a decade and a whole new friendship group to see it.

"The woman who follows the crowd will usually go no further than the crowd. The woman who walks alone is likely to find herself in places no one has ever been before." *– Albert Einstein (or so the internet keeps telling me)*

I hit pretty much rock bottom. Anyone who's been isolated to the point where they are completely alone will understand what I'm getting at. It's shitter than shit. I felt as though the only people I had on my side and who I could talk to were my parents and, as a rebel in her late teens, there was little to no chance of that. Whilst my former pals spent their last summer of schooling attending night clubs, BBQs and garden parties with the rest of our year group, I closed the curtains in my room at 4pm every afternoon and lay in the dark for hours. I was the only student in our school year not invited to the pre-drinks for our 'prom'. I was prescribed anti-depressants and spent my lunch breaks either in the toilet or with the guidance counsellor. Regardless of how stereotypically uncool that makes me sound, she was pretty awesome and sort of saved me in many ways. Immediately after the kick off, I texted both parents to inform them that dropping out of school, four months before my final exams, was my only option. I was never frightened of my peers, but decided it was much better to stay as far away from all drama and subsequent anxiety as possible. I have that wonderful resident counsellor to thank for guiding me back into the land of the living. Basically, I suffered a serious break down as a result of some silly girls who needed entertaining one Sunday afternoon.

At this point, please take at least some comfort in the fact that almost every one of these girls has since approached me, two or three glasses of wine into their night out, and grovelled. And I promise, I'm over it. Like it's not even worth me talking about for longer than 30 minutes in therapy. THAT is how over it I am. And I've forgiven those girls. They were young and stupid and while they said some unforgettable things, it was a different time then. I hope for everyone's sakes that the sisterhood has since found them.

WOMAN UP

Chapter 16

I have anxiety and have battled depression, and I'm a fucking work of art.

Let's put an end to the shame surrounding mental health. There is absolutely nothing to be ashamed of. I know how scary it is to talk about it, or even think about it; but your problems are very, very real. They are valid and deserving of attention and respect. I am someone who doesn't talk about her feelings. As a coping mechanism, I bottle it all up until I'm drunk and emotional and there is an explosion of pain and anger and cheap vodka. I've had full blown arguments with my boyfriend before over text when he was in the same house, because I find it so difficult to talk to someone's face – even someone that I've been courting for years. My first attempt at therapy at age 21 was awful. Much like I do when asked by my family and friends what's wrong, I lied and protested that I was fine. I have an issue with depression which I am learning to control, and pretty severe anxiety which is turning out to be harder than imagined to manage.

I am very good at staying positive, but often find myself living in a bubble or dream world and imagining life to be much rosier than it actually is. And the comprehension of reality hits me just as hard every time. It's not pretty. I also struggle with anger issues and OCD; the combination of which means my reactions are off and often blown completely out of proportion. Do you ever have those days where you just cry for no reason? It's like that, a lot. No one needs to get that irate over one missing spring roll from an M&S party pack. No one needs to hide behind the sofa sobbing because Scotland didn't qualify for the World Cup. I can get worked up and end up completely devastated over something which could be as small as not knowing which shoes to wear for an event.

Hopefully, it will bring you even a portion of the relief it's brought me, to know that I am now in therapy. Proper therapy. Once-a-week-leaving-work-early therapy. And it's working. I feel lighter and like I have someone to talk to who listens and gives a shit and actually helps me. Plus, people keep saying how nice it is to go out with me and not spend the end of their evening worrying about which Nell is going to show up, whether or not I'm going to burst into tears or if they should clear the crockery in case I'm fucked off and need to smash something. It's really only working because it was my idea. I felt like I was ready and it was necessary. And it was! I spent most of my first session twittering about how I wasn't sure I had enough shit going on to warrant weekly counselling. I was obviously wrong. And we've been together ever since. Ain't no love like that between a gal and her therapist, eh?

I don't want to talk to you about my mental illness. I don't want to think of all my darkest moments and spaff them onto this unsuspecting page for you to absorb on your commute or as you drift off before bed, but I'm going to. Because I so wish that, before it consumed me almost entirely, I knew that other people suffered, too. If you're reading this, know that I'm writing on my lunchbreak, hurriedly trying to get the next few paragraphs out so I can go back to not thinking about it again. And if you feel really bad, I will accept PayPal transfers to my wine fund.

My depression has known to be so bad that I struggle to even get out of bed. It feels like I am wearing 26 layers of thick, heavy jackets and I can't stand up straight or walk properly. Whilst it's no-one's fault, it makes me feel as though I hate everyone and the feeling is mutual. It's often a struggle to let my brain prioritize and relax, despite being literally the most organized person ever. Learning to be selfish in ways other than sexually is vital, y'all. When you're feeling overwhelmed, it's absolutely necessary to take a step back. Whatever it is in that moment that seems so enormously insurmountable will pass, I promise.

Pressuring yourself into doing anything that might make matters worse is an unhealthy decision and one to be avoided – I have been known to take time away from work for mental health recovery, and there's no issue in that. Bollocks to anyone who says you can't stay home from work unless you've been struck down with the flu and are on death's door. Your health, regardless of whether that is of body or mind, should be your ultimate priority and taking a day off to deal with that should be regarded as it would if you had the fucking chicken pox. Sit down, have a minute to yourself and just breathe. Learn what it is that induces any feeling of calm, and practice them whenever needs be. This could come from anything from sitting outside with a good book, to a couple of rounds in the boxing ring at your local gym, masturbating in the bath: just do what you can to find your thing and once you've found it, work it into your life whenever and wherever you can.

Soppy, I know, but it also really is OK to be sad. A tricky one, when every second Instagram story tells you that the prettiest girls are the happy ones. Fuck that, and anyone who believes that is the case. I have anxiety and have battled depression, and I'm a fucking work of art. I'm a massively emotional person, and a big crier. I once cried because McDonald's wouldn't serve me a McChicken sandwich during breakfast hours. Admittedly, I was severely hungover and running on only a few hours sleep, but I wept like a baby until they made me my GD sandwich. (I assume this is the same kind of crying blackmail that people use to get out of speeding tickets). We all have bad days. More times than I can count, I've finished work, gone home and cried for hours. Over nothing. Just because it was a shitty Wednesday or it was raining outside or my jeans shrunk in the wash. Like all other emotions, it's vital that you don't bottle them up because if you do, like me, then you'll soon find yourself stood outside in some bar's smoking area, crying until someone has to scoop you up like an infant and take you home. And waking up in the morning with labia lids (swollen eyes after crying look like tiny vaginas on your face) is only going to make you feel worse. So be healthy, watch a sad film or something, and cry it out. Talking about it IS going to help, and trust me, I know that's a whole lot easier said than done. Everyone is going through something, and you might just be able to resonate with whomever it is you share your secrets with.

I have always been terrible with expressing myself. I actually used to believe that I would be dampening the mood or ruining a sunny day if I were to disclose my feelings with friends and actually allow them to meet the inner depths of me. Which doesn't quite add up with how much I cry at literally everything else. My eyes leak for anything other than my feelings in public. I cry at TV adverts, late online shopping deliveries and have been known to bawl over many a book. Present company included. And, in private, I am huge on thinking about those things I rarely touch on and weeping in the shower. But only before getting out, trowelling my face on and facing the world like nothing ever happened.

I have never talked about my feelings. It just doesn't really happen, but I know that I should and I'm working on that. I know that my feelings are real and raw and deserve to be heard and respected; and you should too. It's healthy to discuss your problems and cry it out. It's sooooo not healthy to bottle everything up awaiting inevitable explosion. I'm going to try harder. As much as it cringes me out, I'm going to start honestly answering when people ask me how I am. So, if you enquire and I respond 'fine', make sure you question me on it. Because, more often than not, it's untrue. Not because I'm always unhappy or hurting, mind. Sometimes I use fine because I'm too lazy to say 'really fucking fantastic because this top makes my tits look great and my eggs poached perfectly this morning'.

It will all get better. I once read something that claimed we shouldn't tell people to have a good day when they are feeling sad. Instead, we should simply tell them to have a day. 24 hours of loving and looking after yourself, before re-visiting your feelings tomorrow. Don't give up on yourself; it will get better and, until then, just have a day. You're not the first to go through this, and you won't be the last. We've just got to spread the word that it's OK to talk about mental illness. And that it's OK not to be OK (thanks Jessie J, babes). Feeling and experiencing emotion doesn't mean that you're a bad or undeserving person, it literally just means you're human. You, my dear, are a fucking warrior. You deserve to be happy, and you are not alone.

My particular struggles with mental health have actually contributed to my sex positive discovery. The burger buyer taught me something. The most important relationship you will ever have is with yourself. And whilst I am almost certain that there are other ways to uncover this other than bonking everything that moves, I sure am glad that it is how I came to this conclusion. My relationship with sex completely differs depending on my emotional state. It sounds pretty obvious, but when I'm in a shitty mood, I don't feel good about myself and I am much more likely to put myself in a position to be used. When I'm upbeat and positive, my sex drive is on top form and I want to use the tricks of my trade to seduce everything I come across. I revel in my own glory, and invite others to join me. And I've learned that in comparison to a cheeseburger, the worth of my vagina paired with the rest of the gifts I have to give is comparable to the finest steak, served on a bed of lobster, with a caviar martini on the side. At least.

WOMAN UP

Chapter 17

It is my belief that there is no one great love.
'The One' is make believe.

I wish I could tell you my moderately faulty man-dar improved with age, but that would be a bare faced lie. Ultimately, I became infatuated with chasing men who didn't quite share my feelings, and developed a passion for the turmoil of unrequited love. In all honesty, until I met my current partner, I can't remember a stable relationship in which both my correspondent and I were on the same page. But I did manage to perfect playing it cool when all I really wanted to do was burst into song and propose to the man I'd known for 9 days. I sure know how to pick 'em!

Picking guys who are no good is classic old school Nell. The discovery of sex positivity made it apparent that knowing your worth should be prominent when selecting a mate. Without it sounding too much like a modern day fairytale remake, they're not for you if you're not the best version of yourself when you're with them.

During my last few months of education, a local chap caught my wandering eye. We locked eyes (and eventually, lips) over a pint of lager at a charity quiz night, and the rest was history. Almost. Let me be the first to say that we were never exclusive. If I didn't, I'm almost certain he would chase down every buyer of this book and tell you for himself. Our relationship consisted of a few months of dates, texts and frolicking between the sheets. I have a bit of a problem with falling for people too quickly, and this is a prime example. I slipped, fell and landed right at the feet of 'slow down you're making a biiiiig mistake'. It was easy to fall in love. He was local, meaning I saw him almost everywhere I turned. I lived in a very small town and went out on the same nights, to the same places with the same people, every darn week. Saying this, it was not in my best interests to run into him having just rolled out of bed to fetch breakfast lasagna, dressed in a Groovy Chick dressing gown and blue sequined Ugg boots. After we made eye contact, I actually ran (an incredibly rare occurrence for me) away and hid behind a Royal Mail van.

While I spent my time thinking about how happy he made me, he spent his thinking up excuses and lies to cover up how he really felt. The truth was, he was embarrassed to be with me. I'd gathered somewhat of a reputation about town as a 'serial shagger' (or, again, massive fucking slut), and he struggled to handle the banter that his friends dished out. Unfortunately, said date mate caught wind of how strong my feelings were, and utilized them to satisfy his own needs. He picked me up whenever he or his one eyed trouser snake saw fit, and dropped me the next morning. It was then highly unlikely that I would hear from him again until running into each other at the bar, or the minute his balls started to develop a blue-ish tinge, despite my floods of messages. This resulted in almost two years of chasing. From my part, obviously. And ending the majority of my Friday nights crying into a box of chips, cheese and kebab meat.

There will always be a little soft spot for him somewhere. There's actually a whole lot of soft spots on my body, so I'm not sure which one he is exactly; but I feel for sure that he is there. As I am now a proper sort of grown up woman-child, I don't see him as often. And, when I do, it's nothing but polite and charming. We were friends for a while, but have now dissolved into acquaintances. And, even though I sometimes miss the idea of being on regular speaking terms, it's best for everyone involved this way. We've both moved on. I do feel as though I will always love him, though. Definitely not in the same 'would risk ruining my brand new shoes chasing after him and letting him dump me over and over again' way that I once did, but in some way. Maybe like a brother. Or a close family friend whose penis I've seen one or 100 times. I'm a completely different person now, so all I can do from this point is wish him well in all of his future endeavours. Oh, and advise him to try and not think with his cock and care so much about what other people think.

I want to tell you about our most notable encounter. Mostly because I need to tell someone, so I can stop harbouring the sheer horror and embarrassment and move on with my life, some considerable years later. Yes, it's the moment you've all been waiting for - my first involvement with butt sex. I know what you're thinking – no fairytale ever started with that sentence. The evening had been fuelled with tequila shots and he insisted I stay over. Against my better judgement, I agreed and in an act of bluff, suggested I utilise the guest bedroom. He smugly approved, and took me home. It was inevitable that I wouldn't be alone in the spare room all night, so when he crept in for a 'cuddle', I saw it in my heart to give him one.

And at this point in my book, you can probably guess what 'cuddling' in air quotes means. The tequila hadn't quite worn off so when he accidentally slipped towards my bum hole, I begrudgingly agreed. We were ill prepared and without any form of lubricant, so the discomfort I suffered is imaginable. After he had finished, he retreated back to his own camp and I promptly fell asleep. I was pleasantly surprised to wake up the following morning in what could only be described as a hungover haven. My lover's mother had opted to decorate in various shades of lilac, and clearly taken time and effort with furnishings and what seemed to be a hand crocheted bed spread. Everything was pristine and smelled delightfully fresh, so you can imagine my utter horror when I lifted the covers to get out of bed and was greeted by an angry brown stain the size of a large-ish piece of fruit. Recoiling in horror, I became increasingly aware of the previous night's activities and realisation of where the stain must have come from. A total bummer (…get it).

Kebab baby and inauspicious stain aside, the most stressful part of the whole ordeal was repeatedly bumping into him after I had sworn to get over him. But it happened, and now we are capable of being fully grown adults and seeing each other without the prospect of a drunken fumble or a cry in the toilets. When it all comes down to it, he is a perfectly nice boy, but we were just never suited to be romantically involved. So, if you're looking for a sign – this is it. Come the fuck on, Bridget. Jennifer Anniston got over Brad Pitt and I got over my first love, there's no reason you can't get over the Clio driving knobhead who still lives with his mother. Whilst with one particular devotee, we were able to remain friends post dramatic 'break up', it's frightfully uncommon and not normally healthy to do the same with all.

Living in a small town was hard. Pleasant in the fact that every Friday, even when going to the pub solo, you'd run into a great quantity of people you knew, and could count on leaving with immeasurable memories, but it also meant that I soon grew to know literally everyone. Which inevitably lead to almost all of my sexual partners during that time being ex-boyfriends, past lovers or, indeed, family members of my best friends. Oh, and it meant the entire population knew every sordid detail of my not-so-private life. Not always an ideal situation. And definitely not one best suited for she who bears the green monster almost always. Yeah, I am a proper jealous bitch.

It's not because I'm insecure – I trust my other half and I know he loves me. Without sounding completely arrogant (no change there), my boyfriend is fortunate to have me. I am a catch! I am smart, hilarious and incredibly pretty. Plus I have excellent natural flexibility. Oh, and I make a mean toastie. He's lucky and he knows it. But I just don't trust other people. In classic small town style, I've had 'best friends' go behind my back and shack up with recent exes. To which I've often struggled to respond to in a calm and collected manner. AKA, screaming at each other in the local pub's smoking area. It transpired that she actually double crossed me twice, consecutively, with two separate love interests. I just can't get on board with other people touching what I am touching. This applies to both men and pizza.

It is more than rare to bag yourself a beau with no baggage, small town or no small town. Seriously, everyone has an ex. If not an official ex-boyfriend or girlfriend, then someone they used to hook up with, send dirty snapchats to or chase naked around their parent's garden aged six. And, the older you'll get, the smaller the world will seem. I've moved houses in my life and met entirely new communities of people. Now it's hard to even cross the globe without running into a friend of a friend, yet another ex (of yours or your partner's), or someone who used to date the owner of your cousin's new cat.

It is vital not to get too caught up in anyone's exes. Whilst spending an evening 168 weeks deep into their Instagram might seem like the done thing, persistently mentioning them and wasting your time worrying about them is not. Period. Take it from someone who knows. My jealousy has been known to reach all kinds of levels. Seriously, if my man so much as looks in the direction of the female cashier when he's paying for his petrol, he runs considerable risk of ending up under the wheel, as opposed to behind it. Obviously, I'm joking. But I do look really good in green.

In what will be a surprise to absolutely nobody, as a result of my borderline mentally unstable issues, I often become a little obsessed with the ex. Dating someone new becomes a tormented game of comparison, with hours spent pouring over old pictures of the once happy couple and wondering if the lover between my thighs prefers boobs real or fake. Whilst it's pretty normal to ponder over questions such as; 'will I make him as happy as they did?', 'should I cook for him like they once did' and 'am I better at blowing him than they were?', comparing yourself, in any situation, is unhealthy. As I have harped on a multitude of times, there will only ever be one of you, and you should milk that for all it's worth. Think about it – if your partner didn't think you were worth being with, if they didn't think you were smart, funny or pretty enough, then they wouldn't want to be with you.

It is my belief that there is no one great love. 'The One' is make believe. Sure enough, there are partners best suited to you at different points in your life, but it is rare for one person to be consistent throughout. We change so much over time as individuals, that we have the opportunity for many different loves in our lifetime; each best suited to that particular time in our existence. And those childhood sweethearts who met at 16 and, 30 years later, are still going strong? They've just learned to accept each other's separate changes and differences and grown together. Some of us are destined to have one partner for eternity. Some are meant to be married 14 times. And some are never meant to settle, never meant to be tamed and fated to spend their life thinking of no one but themselves. And that is why relationships take work. And why almost no one has one girlfriend or boyfriend for their entire life. It is your job to find comfort and, ultimately, happiness in any situation.

Breaking up is a natural part of human life. We are not penguins or lobsters or dating in the 1800s, and nothing in our anatomy or mental being promotes seeking only one partner for the duration of our existence. Monogamy isn't natural. And, again, I'm not making an excuse for cheating. Making a commitment to a partner and resisting attraction to other men and women is the first step in even the most basic relationship guidelines. Swearing yourself off anyone else who isn't your lover is what makes you an official couple. And, while being monogamous might not be natural, it's often the most important asset in a healthy non-polyamorous partnership. If you feel a passion, attraction or love for someone stronger than that you hold for your boyfriend or girlfriend, it is time to reassess whether or not you should remain in your relationship.

"I think the idea of marriage is very romantic; it's a beautiful idea, and the practice of it can be a very beautiful thing. I don't think it's natural to be a monogamous person." – Scarlett Johansson

There are hundreds of reasons that two people might chose to end their relationship. And as a result, we have exes. And an ex is just that – the result of a relationship that has come to an end, for a reason. Your current candy and his ex-weren't Romeo and Juliet. Nothing was keeping them apart, they just weren't right for each other at the time. Take comfort in the fact that if your current catch wasn't ready to move on after their ex, the two of you simply wouldn't exist. And, despite wishing that you were the first or only person they'd ever fallen for, you can't change the past.

My boyfriend won't forget his ex; and neither will I. In the beginning of our relationship, I slept in the bed that she once shared with him. Her furniture scattered his house and there were stacks of photo frames with pictures of the two of them, gathering dust in the corner of a room. She moved in similar friendship circles. We've had (slightly awkward) interactions since and, despite some spreading of cringe-worthy and painfully untrue rumours on her part, we've made our peace with the situation and, really, no longer give an ever loving shit. I am a firm believer in ridding your life of both toxic people and toxic situations – which, in this instance, is what both my partner and I have done. I know right, I'm a proper grown up now.

In truth, I have no leg to stand on regarding prior relationships integrating with those currently had. Living in such a small town unfortunately means that regardless of which local haunt my boyfriend and I choose to spend our time, we always run into someone I've dated beforehand. Or shagged; there are a lot of those floating around the UK. Nonetheless, whilst it may bother him to some extent, he never lets my past burden the future we have together. In all honesty, you should be grateful to your significant other's previous lover. They almost definitely contributed in moulding said love interest into the person they are now – and the one you fell in love (or into bed) with.

Chapter 18

You could find me most Sunday mornings, strutting down the high street with last night's mascara under my eyes, high heels in hand and a big old I've-just-been-shagged smile on my face.

Since before I can remember, and I mean way back when, I have had a slight obsession with rugby players. And by slight I mean a full blown, Facebook stalking, serious infatuation. And it's not even the game; just uber muscly thighs and boys who won't text me back. In my early teens, I developed a serious adoration for the Australian international team, and one particularly young and handsome, bleached blonde player (there's a pattern here somewhere…). I thought I was the shit back then (who are we kidding, I still do), and honestly believed that as soon as the clock struck midnight on my 18th birthday, I would be shipped off to The Gold Coast to find and immediately wed this young rugby player. Thankfully, and although it took a good few years, I got over my crush and succumbed to the fact that he was actually probably going to marry the girlfriend that he had already been courting for five years. But it's nice to look back on the overwhelming confidence and hope that no doubt stood me in good stead for years to come. Especially considering I was 15 years old, with a penchant for only brushing my hair once every two weeks and fake-tanning my lower limbs until they looked like giant cheesy wotsits.

Mid-fascination, my dad managed to bag us some tickets to watch my golden boys play England in the Autumn Internationals. I was like a fan girl on steroids, and watched the game through happy, tear-filled eyes and various bouts of springing out of my seat for a picture with any passing player. He then surprised me with a pass to the players bar, where I met the full squad for both sides and could have died in ecstasy right then and there. Bar going to see the S Club 7 reunion tour, it still stands as the best day of my life. Don't grow up, it's a trick.

My dad played rugby professionally, so I happened to spend a chunk of my life growing up surrounded by his fellow playmates. So, really, it was only natural for me to develop a love for the sport and those who play it. And so, having binned off my floppy haired bleach blonde surfer boy phase, I started working my way through my local club. As aforementioned, I gained somewhat of a 'reputation' through my social life and endeavours. And, to no-one's surprise, this propagated through my antics at the rugby club. I bedded a number of them, and regretted none.

Some, I would repeat. I had a particular liking for a certain few who I knew were consistent following a few pints of Guinness and the decision to ignore their fellow player's 'banter'. I envisioned a future with one particular conquest, but soon learned the hard way that it's virtually impossible to shag your way to love. And, so I ditched the idea of happily ever after and opted for Mr Right Now over Mr Right – initiating contact on those Saturday nights when Gashley and I needed some attention. By the way, Gashley is the name of my vagina. Man-cycling isn't a crime, and if most of the men we know are doing it; why can't women? How many times have you been interested and then let down by a man, only to have him re-instate contact when he needed something (more often than not, to get his dick wet)?

Getting to know someone can be difficult and really darn infuriating. Particularly if using dating sites and apps to source your suitors; conversing with potentials without doing so in person can be an absolute nightmare. We live in a social society – where almost all communicating is done via smart phone. All too often your classic dating app matches you with someone aesthetically divine, only to discover that, in person, their chat is downright pants. It's virtually impossible to properly get to know someone via 4G. Emotions, sarcasm and tone of voice can't be translated through a keyboard - no matter how many Emojis you use, and, without thoroughly understanding their conversation, you're less than likely to wish to pursue a face to face meet. So, before you know it, you've landed back at square one and you're liking the latest Instagram post of someone you snogged on a night out that one time. JUST to get a reaction. And maybe, if you're lucky, a text.

Small talk alongside (less than) original pick-up lines is the bane of single gal existence. Does anyone frequently yearn to spend their Tuesday evenings discussing jobs, family and where they enjoy socialising or previous holiday destinations with someone they swiped that morning? In all honesty, I'd rather lay in bed watching The Real Housewives of literally anywhere and eating my way through the tin of shortbread that my Nan gifted me in 2016. While I strongly believe it is wrong to lead someone on under false pretences, it doesn't fall into the same ball park to 'catch up' with a prior bed-sharer to kill a little boredom or fill the chunky, rugby player-shaped hole in your life. Sometimes you just need entertaining from someone who knows you - or a sext from someone who is familiar with your inner kink.

I guess this is the theory behind the 'Little Black Book'. In my case, it was less little and black and more A4 and bright pink. Didn't you know? Subtle is my middle name. It's become the obviously weird mark of a true bachelor to have a pocket-sized diary detailing the women he's previously slept with/courted. You remember seeing Joey in *Friends* scouring through said book to find Phoebe a date? Only to discover it was filled with the phone numbers and home addresses of unsuspecting girls. And *How I Met Your Mother's* smooth-talking Barney Stinson has an endless stream of females he habitually refers to. What kind of double standard allows for men to be defined as stud-like by keeping their exes details and further using them, but for a woman to recycle a man, it would no doubt be labelled pathetic or desperate? Riddle me this - if we aren't allowed to revisit ex flames and dig up past dirt then why do Facebook have a relationship status for 'It's Complicated'? Isn't it always?

One gent in particular sparked my interests over a series of nights out and a fair few weeks of admiration. He ticked all physical boxes on my then 'boyfriend must have' list and was well over six foot, and built like a brick shit house. He was bloody gorgeous, covered in tattoos and could make my fanny flutter from a mile off. Out one Friday evening, we began to enter territory that was cosier than our usual cuddle at the bar. My trusty friends warned me that, owing to the size of him and his perpetually aggressive persona, he would 'ruin' me. I was nothing short of excited and beyond ready to be drilled by a Pacific Islander the size of a family Land Rover.

Anyway, to cut a painfully long story short, he was the master of a micro penis. Normally, I wouldn't mind. I've been up close and personal with a lot of mini members, and worked with what I was given, ending with what I hope was perfectly satisfactory shagging for all involved parties. But, seeing as the size of your dick isn't synonymous with how good you are in between the sheets, I expect effort and willing from any and all parties involved. In this case? There was no effort. And no party. In my pants or otherwise.

Initially, after the shock realisation that the thing was actually in, I offered a variation of different positions and techniques to try and stimulate a mutually beneficial love making, but, alas, he was not interested. Instead, he proceeded to continue his selfish sex quest, ignoring my poor, physically and emotionally empty vag until he produced his love liquor and rolled over to instantaneously begin snoring.

My London stint was a hotbed for rugby players. I started only dating rugby playing men, changing my Tinder bio to say just that, and then quickly decided that I would instead only offer my time and expensive lingerie to anyone playing in the premiership and then, you've guessed it, swore to only allow myself to be bought dinner and penetrated by those with an international cap. I normally pride myself on my high standards, but this all went considerably downhill from that terrible decision making on my part. I use the term hot bed very literally because after one had crawled out of mine, it wasn't long before another rolled in. I was in my element - My Whatsapp and Facebook messenger were brimming with wankers, looking for an easy lay and all geared up to take me for a burger – providing it would lead to the removal of my knickers. And, plot twist, it nearly always did.

The thing is with professional sportsmen, is that they are constantly bred and pumped full of the belief that they are the shit, and no one else comes close. Their careers are highly competitive and, especially with a sport like Rugby, they have a sort of understanding that regardless of how many times they've made it onto the tele, there are always going to be people supporting and cheering for them, and women waiting for their go as the latest, most glamorous Rugby wag. It was a completely different league to any that I'd dated in before. On more than one occasion I was taken on a multitude of dates (lots of burgers and not a lot of knicker-wearing) only to discover, months down the line, that my wooer was actually not at all single. And, often, engaged or even married. Obvs I'm not really into being a side dish (do I look like garlic bread to you?), and so never hung around after such revelations.

It would be stating the obvious to claim I've been intimate with a lot of rugby players, but what can I say? There's just something about the way they carry those oddly shaped balls.

For me, my single Oxfordshire years are defined by drinking locally and even many wobbly evenings at the rugby club, hoping to pull. I had a pretty high success rate and, despite how much their teasing and referring to me behind my back as the club bike, they kept crawling back for more. And sure, this is probably because they thought I was easy. But more fool them, I was alert and ready to squirt, happily shagging around and quite frequently bagging myself a new t-shirt or hoodie the next morning. You could find me most Sunday mornings, strutting down the high street with last night's mascara under my eyes, high heels in hand

and a big old I've-just-been-shagged smile on my face. I was not to be phased by harsh words and scathing looks; I will stand as a proud slut for the rest of my life. Hold the phone whilst I get that copyrighted and tattooed...

By the time I met my current boyfriend, he had been warned off me by a multitude of the rugby club's community. Not those who had actually bedded me prior, but the players and girlfriends who had decided that I was not to be liked as a result of my healthy and happy sex life. Did I happen to mention how judgemental and slut-shame-y my hometown is?

Whilst they might have beat around my bush, I'm not going to this time, and I'm not going to tell you all that actually I was wrong and rugby players are dreamy and the epitome of the strong, manly spouse that your parents imagined you ending up with. Equally, I'm not going to warn you off them – I've found an amazing one, and I'm sure, with enough of a thorough search and process of elimination, you could too. But my experience with sportsmen has generally been of similar ilk.

Rugby players are tricky, and often just that – players. But, honey, so is almost every other man. I'm not here to worsen reputations, but should you find yourself ghosted after an evening of rucking, don't say I didn't warn you.

Chapter 19

Regardless of how idyllic it sounds, don't have sex on the beach. Sunsets are romantic, sand in your fanny is not.

I am a child of the sun. Holidays are my fave and, having spent my childhood traipsing around Spain's 25 most famous churches, my idea of a vacay nowadays consists of a lot of large cocktails - hold the tail.

I would much rather opt for a bikini, book and beach rather than chronic thigh chafe and a brood of whinging siblings. As a fully grown adult-style woman, my holidays are now ones that, more often than not, my parents have paid for and I have chosen to tag along. Listen, it's hard to fork out for a week in Croatia when your rent is half your monthly wage and Zara keep having sales.

Before we continue, let me explain what I mean by 'child of the sun'. I essentially mean that if there's a cool breeze and a pool close by, I can stay in the sun all day long, happily sipping on sangria and reading the totality of Caitlin Moran's published works and those biographies I was harping on about. But, straight sun and no breeze/way of cooling myself down, and I begin to physically melt, Wicked Witch of the West style. I become moist in all the wrong ways, and have to keep nipping into the safety of the cool indoors every half an hour. I don't bode well in the heat.

Why is it that, when going on holiday, you always envision yourself as a brand new, tranquil and not at all shrill person, indulging in only the finest fresh produce and fully engulfing yourself in every aspect of a new culture? Oh, the things you will do and the people you will meet. But, instead, it always transpires that rather than the romantic, cocktail infused rooftop terrace evening you'd pictured, you find yourself in the same position every evening – lying naked on the bed, eating Lays.

I've actually only been on one full blown girls' holiday. And, considering the amount of away-from-home shagging I've done, that's an achievement. So, yes, I've done a lot of sunshine sexing when on my holibobs with my parents. And no, I have no shame. I actually had to sneak someone out of our Portuguese villa one year, in a rapid attempt to hide him from the prying eyes of my four brothers. It's a damn shame that children get up so early. Getting him out and through the automatic gate system was an expedition in itself. In the end, I managed to give him a leg up and over the fence. So, my little brothers didn't get to meet my conquest. But they did stumble across me, sweaty and out of breath, leaning against the hedge after an activity more strenuous than the bonking itself.

My first ever holiday romance (awwww) was at the tender age of 13. We were on a resort-type holiday with the full family, and all three of us offspring (PD – pre divorce) were booked into Kid's Club. Do imagine my fury when I learnt that, just three weeks later I would have been 14, and therefore allowed into the 'teen' section, where my beloved heart's desire spent his days. Again, I was barely a teen, and so, whilst we did actually have a few romantic moments alone on the beach together (I even touched his hand), our relationship was mostly me watching him from behind a canoe and giggling with the other girls who hadn't quite made it into teenage heaven.

Don't get me wrong, I was in no way mature or sensible enough to understand relationships or pine after a floppy haired, rash vest wearing fuckboy-to-be. My parents were right to keep me in the same club as my baby sister. I seem to remember that, after spending my days lusting after rash vest boy and re-adjusting my tankini to perfectly show off my new henna tattoo, each evening I crawled into bed with my cuddly giraffe and an overwhelming sense of innocence.

I took a ski trip with my family and some friends back in the initial stages of my hoe phase. I was at an age where I desperately pretended to be grown up, but was still very much immature. By day, I would sing Disney songs up and down the chair lifts and by night, would sip on double gins, stumbling around in my enormous faux fur coat. In my mind, I was channelling the look of sexy Russian royalty, but in reality, I looked like a drunk Furby. A friend of mine was doing a season nearby, so one evening I made sure to stop by for an enormous pint or four. The evening ended with us shagging over the toilet in the en-suite to my hotel room, where my sister was asleep in our bed. Just in case anyone has been left wondering, there is nothing sexy about riding someone on a loo. The holiday overlapped New Years, and I ended up bedding another new acquaintance. Again, it would be wrong to refer to it as 'bedding' as I watched the midnight fireworks whilst being bent over a windowsill in the boot room of his hotel. Say what you want, but it was nice to see the New Year in with a bang.

Does it count as a holiday romance if I was back in the area of Scotland where I grew up, shagging people I used to know? Yeah? Cool! Then I've had a fair few of those. One ex-acquaintance offered to kindly pick me up from the train station after a girl's night in Edinburgh. And so naturally I repaid him with a shag in his car overlooking the poshest golf course in the area. I revisited said golf course during the same trip. This time with a different boy, and for some casual cunnilingus. That is until I heard a frog and scarpered back to the house party that we'd escaped from. On a side note, there seems to be a recurring pattern of me trading 20-25 minutes of boning for the most simple of favours. I should probably make a mental note to discuss this with someone professional.

I'd often use visiting Edinburgh and the neighbouring towns as an excuse to shack up with anyone who I'd either deemed fit from afar or had been texting/sexting with. Obviously I opt not to do this anymore, given that I am in a committed and loving long-term relationship. But I struggle to remember a time (during my single years) when visiting my home town, that I haven't jumped into bed with a kilt-wielding Scot. Nothing has re-enforced my love for this incredible city quite like doing the stride of pride down The Royal Mile. Some of them were pretty damn memorable. Scotch Beef, for one. No, for real; he was an ex-model and had once been the face of Scotch Beef at the high point in his career. He was tall and handsome and lured me into bed (not that it took any convincing at all) with his soft Scottish accent and very cool demeanour. Oh, and the pictures that I found of him modelling kilts during an extensive Google search made me wetter than an otter's pocket.

After that, my Scottish shags had to work hard to compete. During the same trip, which happened to be a pre-Christmas girls weekend where everyone ended up bringing their boyfriends, leaving me and the one other single gal enjoying the sights and sounds of Edinburgh (whisky and handsome men), I met with another of my pre-trip pen pals. He played rugby. Seriously, that's all I remember. Obviously there's some switch in my brain which automatically turns itself off after egg chasing is mentioned. Anyway, he picked me up from a night out and, with a necessary stop for two battered sausages and a portion of chips, took me back to his flat.

If you think men are gross, prepare yourself for sportsmen. Their flat shares and homes are honestly more disgusting than public toilets frequented by vermin. They don't pick up or clean anything after use and, weirdly, none of them ever use a bathmat. Oh, and this particular living space didn't have sheets, duvet covers or pillow cases on any of the beds. Just naked, scratchy surfaces which meant I spent most of my night lying as still as possible so as not to catch my leg stubble on the fibres. Well, that and being vigorously and sporadically rumped for four seconds at a time. I spent the spells dreaming about the half a sausage that I knew had been left on the kitchen side. Still, to this day I often wonder how long it was left there before consumed or binned. Miss you, babe.

My most memorable holiday romance, should you be so inquisitive, was one of my first ever double dates. I was around 16, and we were vacationing with extended family in a place called Sorrento. It was beautiful, and is one of the reasons for my complete adoration of all things Italian. There's something about being in a country famous for wine, carbs and romance that really ticks my boxes. When I visited Rome, I fell so in love that I came fairly close to chaining myself to The Vatican in a bid to never leave. But then I realised I'd have to live the rest of my days with my knees covered, and I wasn't quite so keen. During this particular summer, at this particular hotel, there just so happened to be an incredibly adorable waiter. Picture him as the 19 year old Italian answer to Chris Pine. I spent the first few days of my break sitting by the pool and watching him carry out his day-to-day jobs over the top of my sunglasses and one of E.L James's works. Admittedly, I was probably hard to ignore, considering most days I wore a sun hat to rival the size of Jupiter, and have a laugh so loud that Vesuvius itself trembled whenever I opened my mouth. Whatever I did worked though, and before long he was bringing me complimentary iced teas.

One evening at dinner, he actually asked my aunt and uncle (thinking they were my parents) if he could take me out the following evening. After fluttering my eyelashes and politely accepting his most gracious request, he then extended the invitation to one of my cousins, as one of his fellow handsome waiters quite fancied the look of her. So, we went out. It was next level exciting for a virgin whose male interaction level had only previously reached smiling at the handsome shoe-fitter in her local sports shop. They drove us into the town in a vintage Fiat 500 and we spent the evening sat in a tiny little local terrace bar, sipping mojitos.

It was oh so romantic and the terrace was adorned with twinkling fairy lights wrapped around trunks of the orange trees that masqueraded as our roof. Anyway, I was sitting there in my pretty little dress being all funny and clever and flirty and assuring myself that I looked exactly like Audrey Hepburn in Roman Holiday, when a whopping great mouldy orange descended from one of the trees, landed and exploded on my head. I was now considerably sticky, fucking mortified and wearing bits of old orange in my hair and all over my expertly selected outfit. Honestly, I've never experienced anything like it. And obviously neither had they, as almost everyone around me cascaded into utter hysterics, leaving me sour (and sticky) faced with a major sense of humour failure. Despite how much I tried to laugh it off, the incident had somewhat sobered me up and I left shortly after, smelling like a walking air freshener.

The truth is, holiday romances are tricky! Those feelings of lust and passion that you were so overcome with whilst writhing around in the sand are seldom the same once back in your rainy homeland. Don't get me wrong – I've read and experienced testimonials where people have met their future spouse at Ocean Beach Ibiza or queueing for the Colosseum in Rome, but they've got to be the exception to the rule. Something strange seems to happen when travelling overseas. The cocktails get stronger and the sun must have some peculiar effect on your brain, because you start to consider people who, if you'd met playing darts in your local, you'd avoid like the plague. Maybe it's something to do with holidays generally relaxing all of our senses, but, within a few days in the sun, you'll soon find yourself imagining life shacked up on a Greek island with your bartender, Nico.

Vacationing impairs your judgement. Everything is exciting and adventurous – including being fingered by an 18-year-old pool boy behind the outdoor changing area. I mean, I totally get it. Just thinking about it, I'm getting a little turned on (holiday romances, and not the 18-year-old boy). The thought of balmy evenings, exotic food and strange and glamorous languages makes me want to cash my EasyJet points in as a matter of urgency.

Obviously I'm a firm ambassador for doing what you want, and that doesn't stop here. Shag the bartender. Go home with the gorgeous local that you keep bumping into. Take advantage of the lack of shot measurers in Europe, and pass out drunk spooning your mate and her beau. Just don't get your hopes up that your fling will immediately want to wed you. Don't listen to your friends after more than two margaritas, and, regardless of how idyllic it sounds, don't have sex on the beach. Sunsets are romantic, sand in your fanny is not.

WOMAN UP

Chapter 20

There's no better declaration of love than nine pancakes in one sitting.

Believe it or not, I'm far from a hopeless romantic. I mean, the odd candle lit dinner doesn't go amiss and I like to kiss on the mouth before fucking, but I don't get giddy over chocolates and giant teddy bears and I'm not overly crazy about Valentine's Day. Whilst I'm not a huge believer, I do hold some enjoyment for buying hideously inappropriate cards for my partner, and receiving declarations of love in return. Before I met my lovely man friend, I celebrated Galentine's Day – just like V Day, but with your gal pals and copious amounts of your chosen alcohol. We had so much fun, and these celebrations are a reminder of how important it is to celebrate all relationships in your life – not just those that fall into category: romance.

Galentine's Day is always a blast. Sure, V Day is great if you're into red roses and romance, but the original G Day will forever hold a place in my heart as the best ever February 14th. Considering the exclusivity of the event and the fact that there are a dozen of us in my girl group (meaning it's suuuper hard to get us all in the same place at once), even our friends who were in couples at the time sacked off their other halves for a girls day and night. We saw the debut of the first 50 Shades in the cinema, and followed it up with a stomach-lining Noodle Bar. But the night out was by far the highlight of our 24 hours. We drank Oxford dry of vodka lime and sodas and danced the night away. It was delightful. Of course, ignoring the small mishap that was me attempting to relieve myself behind some bins by the Thames, slipping, falling and skidding about 20ft on my arse. In hindsight, it's probably a good thing that I didn't notice until the next morning, the fact that my brand new, pristine, white bodycon skirt was ruined forever. Thankfully, my dear friend who had escorted me couldn't talk from laughing so much and so couldn't have told me either.

Aside from celebrating the relationships with your friends and if Gal/Palentine's Day doesn't do it for you; each and every year, I encourage the revelling of 'Me Day', rather than V/G/P Day. The celebration and preservation of the relationship that should always come first in life – with yourself. Loving yourself is vital. I've heard people saying that you can't be loved until you love yourself which, quite frankly, is bollocks. People will always love you – happy or sad, big or small, self-loving or self-loathing. Please don't pin shitty threats like that on other people's issues. What stands in the way of relationships when you don't love yourself, is just that – yourself. It is difficult to fully open yourself to be loved when you are self-conscious and afraid of being vulnerable.

Try and sidestep boyfriend bonfires and playing Miss Havisham, Valentine's Day is no excuse to wallow in self-pity and prise open the ex-files. Celebrate love in all of its glory. There are many ways to practice self-love, not just on greetings card holidays, but always. On 'Me Day', why not treat yourself? Often, my favourite gifts are those labelled 'To Me, From Me'. Personally, when I'm really treating myself, I will do so by splurge on something ridiculous and completely unnecessary, like a USB desk hoover, or Hello Kitty shaped plasters. I am 25 and paying rent in Oxfordshire, so there's no chance in this world that I would be able to afford a spa day. But, if you could, that might be a nice idea. Oh, how the other half live.

If, like me, you've spent the remainder of your savings on miniature desktop cleaning products, then there's no great Saturday night quite like one spent in your dressing gown, inhaling the chocolates that you got reduced on February 15th and cackling with laughter as you watch Bridesmaids for the 107th time.

'Alentine's Ay' has been hailed as the holiday for those who won't be getting the 'V' or 'D' on Valentine's Day. I mean, 2019 was my fourth February 14th in a committed relationship; and I didn't see his penis once. The first we spent together, we both endured an hour long argument following my other half's refusal to order me a kebab, so we've never been your traditionally romantic couple. Being brutally honest, my idea of the perfect date is receiving top notch oral sex while stuffing my face with mac n cheese balls, online shopping with his credit card and watching the entire *Girls* box set. I'm not really one for dating - my wheelie bin goes out more than I do. I'm more a 'stay at home with Netflix and gin' kind of dater. A 'cheap date', you might say, but that entirely depends on how much Chinese food I'm in the mood for.

When my fella and I organize date nights (we do that on days not in mid-February, too, sometimes…) we like to opt for a really early dinner or movie, to make extra double sure that we are home in time for a good hour or so snuggled up on the sofa before heading to Bedfordshire for the necessary eight hours.

Working yourself up over not having a date for this greeting card holiday is pointless. Almost as pointless as actively recruiting a partner purely for such an occasion. Trust me, this almost never works out and all too often leaves you in a sticky situation, stuck between a cock and a hard place. Following so soon post-crimbo, the big V is a welcome occasion to catch up on some well-deserved pampering. Give yourself a pedicure to show off in the peep toes you've treated yourself to. Spend the day exfoliating every inch if you are so inclined, either in preparation for your big night out or cosy night in and, should you truly be invested in anti-Valentine's, take inspo from Jessica Biel in the namesake movie and throw you and your single pals a party. Or, if that's not your kind of thing – find an alternative. It really is just about doing something for yourself.

Celebrating self-love evokes the opportunity to properly show yourself some attention. By yourself I mean your crotch and by attention I mean furious masturbation. And what better an excuse! After you've been suitably self-satisfied, you can begin sharing the love. Not necessarily necking on with your BFF after an abundance of tequila (which, coincidentally, is always an appropriate option), but by making sure your loved ones know just how loved they are. From then you're free to crank up Cardi B, and forget about 'loving' your toes as you twerk your way into February 15th.

Admittedly, I celebrated 'Me Day' this year with both my boyfriend and my mother, and continued my Shrove Tuesday festivities long into the 14th. There's no better declaration of love than nine pancakes in one sitting. This year was the first of the new agreement between my partner and I, to not give or receive physical luxuries (other than the annual card that I receive from my Father) and, instead, give the very much sought after gift of my love and company. That lucky, lucky bastard.

Oh the subject of make believe holidays, I should probably address the issue of the fantasy day that falls just a month afterwards. 'Steak and Blowjob Day', much like its mainstream and more romantic cousin 30 days prior, has not got me convinced. I like my steak rare and my blowjobs as short and inconsistent as possible. Don't get me wrong, I love sex. I am fully pro sex, very sex positive and there's honestly no other pastime I'd rather engage in. To me, there's no finer idea than staying in for the evening with a delicious meal and a delicious man. If Steak and Blowjob day was this, a mutually beneficial celebration of a couple's love for one another, then I would be on my knees quicker than you could say 'fellatio' – but I'm just not convinced that that is the case.

Isn't it just another holiday made up by entitled white men who think women owe them something? According to myth, legend and LadBible, it falls exactly one month after Valentine's Day because men feel like they have done sooooooooooo much for their other halves on ONE day of the year (how much effort does a Moonpig card and a box of chocolates really take, though?) that they deserve oral pleasure and a lump of expensive meat. Lest we forget all that we do for our partners every other day of the year. For me, personally, I know I spend the majority of my free time washing dirty boxer shorts and putting the toilet seat down after my certain someone. It's a fucking Christmas miracle that Chicken and Lickin' Day isn't more popular.

Apparently, Valentine's Day has become a commercial holiday for women, because men do not like or want stereotypical 'V Day' gifts such as flowers, chocolates, teddy bears etc. Not only is this wholly gender stereotypical and pretty damn sexist but also totally incorrect. For starters, who doesn't like chocolate?! If we didn't buy you your own, you know you'd only end up eating ours anyway. Plus, without stating the very obvious, this is a stupid statement. For V Day this year, I got my boyfriend a card, a celebratory Burger King dinner and an evening of anal play. AKA, his dream Wednesday evening. Valentine's Day is for celebrating love, and not exclusively the love that a man has for a woman.

Men do NOT need another day to inflate their egos or make them feel more entitled than they already do. If I had the time and there was less dirty rugby washing to do, I could sit and list the things that women do for men that are taken for granted (the idea of growing their offspring and pushing a human out of their vagina springs to mind). And do we sit and moan, whining and asking for a day of misogynistic celebration? No.

The be all and end all is this – gifts and affection shouldn't be given with the idea that they will then owe you the same. If your relationship bears this brunt, then you've got more to worry about than going tit-for-tat on Hallmark holidays.

WOMAN UP

Chapter 21

Sex is sex, and rape is rape.

Following those wasted two years that I fatefully spent chasing he who was afraid of commitment and banter, I finally moved on and briefly dated a military man. Specifically, a Royal Marine. I use the term 'briefly' in the loosest way possible, as I was head over heels within a few weeks. It wasn't much of a regular position as he was based somewhere near Portsmouth, but he ventured back every few weekends to provide me with severe sexual satisfaction. Well worth the fortnightly wait.

Retrospectively, I was foolish not to have clocked on to his antics beforehand. He never spoke about his social life, and infrequently allowed me to discuss let alone socialise with his friends. He would disappear on nights out with the promise of returning home to me, and become MIA for days at a time. Unsurprisingly, I was not the only inkpot that he was dipping his pen in. One fateful Valentine's Day I hosted something of an after party following our weekly Friday antics at the local pub. This basically translates into seven to ten people, drinking my dad's beers and stuffing themselves full of kebab meat before promptly passing out on my couch. To this particular sought after event, I had invited one of my old school friends. We caught up and ended up excitedly discussing the fact that we were both courting Marines. You guessed it - it was the same guy and, after calling him out, I was treated to a live snapchat of the two of them shagging. A real pleasantry to open over breakfast with my grandparents.

Whilst I wish it could have been different, not all of my sexual encounters have been easy. It takes a whole lot for me to put this into words, and months of avoiding editing just these paragraphs. I am not telling you these stories for sympathy. I am letting my voice be heard in hope that it inspires other voices who might have be silenced or shamed.

At 18, I was locked in a Travelodge suite, not far from home, and tortured by a (different, but equally as horrible) marine. He ripped my clothes and refused to let me leave without the performance of certain sexual favours. Thankfully, I was able to escape and retreat to my parked car. He followed me, of course, and rode with a petrified me until I quite literally kicked him to the kerb somewhere between junctions four and five on the M40. Two years later, I was raped.

Sexual assault is something I have been threatened with for a long time. In no malicious way, mind. But at various points in my life, having grown concerned, those who care about me have stated that should I carry on behaving in such a way (basically, sleeping with whomever I wish and whenever I wish) people would get the wrong impression and I would end up a victim. In a slightly twisted way, that is exactly what happened. It was a desperately vain attempt to make my then love interest jealous, and I invited one of his teammates for dinner. Dinner, we had. Half a bottle of wine, we had. Consensual sex? We did not have. In truth, I was mortified. Everything that my friends and family had warned me would happen, finally did. Subconsciously, I let it eat away at me. I was exhausted, angry and humiliated, which lead to two weeks spent bedbound, signed off work on 'compassionate leave'.

I was embarrassed to the point where even the thought of confessing to someone made my stomach turn. And I am a woman who has no shame. Often, I would wake up and think it just a dream. I played the evening on repeat in my head until I convinced myself, multiple times, that it had been my fault. Until I was once again crippled by the cruel reality. Before long, it was becoming so unhealthy for me to keep such a secret that I was forced to confide in a friend. Without a release, I would have imploded. I sat aside her before a night out, barely holding myself together as I brushed over the events of two weeks prior. Unfortunately, on that same night, I came face to face with my abuser once more. Of all the nightclubs in all of London, he happened to stumble into the one where I was drowning my sorrows with copious amounts of sparkler topped, watered down vodka. In case you haven't experienced it yet, the mixture of alcohol, panic and pain is not one to be reckoned with. It was within an hour that, having complained to the bouncer and been verbally abused by his friends, we were shown the door after a swift nod from his direction. It was a short while before I could scrape myself off the Kings Road and agree to retreat to bed. Regrettably, the slightly hysterical scene that I caused now meant that everyone knew. My friends, my father and a fair few residents of Chelsea.

I sat on it for another week before eventually going to the police. Six months of frequent panic attacks, a fortnight out of work and a bout of therapy and my case was declined as a result of having slept with his teammates. Consensually. After dating them (separately) for months. Reportedly, the fact that I kept a blog detailing my dating and sex life didn't help, either. I had obviously forgotten that writing about normalising sex is a definite invitation for anyone to use my body as they so wish.

I wish I could tell you it gets easier, and one day you stop thinking about it; but I can't. What I can say, however, is something like this - any form of sexual assault is never the victim's fault. No amount of alcohol, short skirts, low cut tops and previous sexual history can be used to excuse anyone who commits sexual assault.

Consent is mandatory. It really is that simple. And yet it is baffling that we still have to tell people not to have sex with anyone else against their will. Sex is sex, and rape is rape. No means no. Unsure about how your partner feels regarding sex? Don't do it. If they've had a little too much to drink and cannot fully consent? Don't do it. If they agreed initially and then changed their mind? Don't fucking do it. It really is that simple.

Modern society's concept of rape is worryingly old fashioned. It is time we ended rape culture, once and for all. Rape culture demonstrates the ways in which society blames victims of sexual assault and normalizes male sexual violence. It is frequently preached about via social media, though we are still teaching our children how not to be raped, rather than teaching them not to rape. So, let's get this straight. Non consensual sex, under any circumstances, is not acceptable. Consent is the word 'yes'. It is verbal willingness. Anything else - silence, physical or verbal refusal, unconsciousness, anything, is not. If your partner initially decides to engage in sexual activity, and then changes their mind, that is not consent. If there is any doubt in your mind that the human you are about to be intimate with might not reciprocate your feelings, you should not even question whether you should proceed. The insidious influence of rape culture is to blame for the 94.3% of accused abusers who will never face a conviction.

"There remains what seems like an impenetrable wall of silence around violence and we must all play a role in breaking this silence." – Reese Witherspoon

Let's talk about it a little more often. Let it be known that violence and sexual assault on any level is categorically unacceptable. I won't let him take away my dignity, and I won't let him ruin my life. I am not weak because this happened to me; I am grown and stronger and ready to fight for anyone who's been in my position.

I am tired of sexual harassment scandals – and I know it's easy to sit at home and type that. But, seriously, how can we still be justifying their behaviour when 10, 20 and even hundreds of women are coming forward and speaking out about what happened to them at the hands of someone unexpected. Trust me, I know that speaking up and actually discussing it is fucking hard. That's partly why I chose to tell all here. Still, unless I am many a vino in, I can't say the R word without feeling physically sick.

In the moment, my friends were incredibly supportive. They sat with me as I was questioned time and time again by the police, and made surprise visits to my home bringing flowers, cream cakes and milkshakes. They would ask me, gently because they know what I'm like, how I was doing and checked up on me daily. For a few days after going to the police, I was fine. And then very suddenly and very intensely I was not. I couldn't be around people who weren't my close friends and family without having crippling anxiety attacks. This meant that work was out of the question, hence the signing off. And then everyone forgot. Not about me, but about my pain and what I was dealing with internally. And I don't blame them.

My mum and dad are not bad people. I love them, and I know they love me. We've had our ups and downs, but I know now that inevitably they will always be there for me. But their reaction to what happened to me just cemented how considerable the generational gap is surrounding issues like these. Naturally and initially, my dad was furious. If you paid attention to the third chapter, you'll know how protective Daddy Grecian can be. We have a very close relationship, so I imagine he was also disappointed that I chose not to confide in him. In the years since, I haven't even spoken properly to my mum about it. Honestly, I don't know why. Considering, I tell her literally everything else, including the lengthy details of some oddly placed skin tags, the idea of us having a secret not shared is alien. And, sure, like everyone else born of a similar era, Ma and Pa are pretty old fashioned when it comes to stuff like this.

Their generation are literally the opposite of sex-forward. Sex-backwards? I don't know. Regardless, I found out about two years later that, after years of warning me about 'this kind of thing', they struggled to process everything that had happened and, in turn, unleashed their frustrations on an unsuspecting me. I was told that I really shouldn't have invited him over to an empty house if I didn't want him to expect something. Sorry, what? How about women don't owe men anything, and if I wanted to invite him over for some fucking stir fry and to watch a film from opposite ends of the sofa, then that should have been no issue.

In no way do I accuse them of endorsing rape culture and victim blaming. Insensitive, yes, and definitely confused; but they (and it has since been confirmed) were never trying to contribute to my pain, only appropriately deal with theirs. And like I said, this is precisely why we need to bridge the gap and educate everyone on how it is. I'm not going to pick faults with my parents; nobody is perfect and for them to have raised Satan's spawn, they each deserve to be bought an island. But it was shit. I felt as though all of my deepest insecurities and constant self-doubts about my rape were being effectuated by my parents. AKA, the people that are meant to love me unconditionally and always be there to pick up the pieces and hold my hair back when I'm chundering my life away. In true Nell style, I've voiced these concerns to them now, multiple times over, and usually after a heavy day session and an impressive consummation of cheese sandwiches.

Then came my first stint in therapy. You remember, the one that failed miserably. I just wasn't very good at it. I tried to talk about what happened and how I felt, and failed miserably. When I had my second session (which in turn became my last) I was adamant that I was fine, and that I probably didn't need therapy anymore. I was not fine, and clearly, still in need of therapy.

I honestly think everyone does. There are so many issues in this world that could be solved by sitting, discussing and thinking rationally about your own problems. Yes, it's totally hypocritical for me to say this, as I've only really just started to take my own advice and learn to heal through actively talking about what happened. Sober. And not being so scared of burdening people with my problems and feelings.

WOMAN UP

Chapter 22

There's really no reason to cry over spilt semen.

My 'crazy' current girlfriend status (ironic considering I've only been blessed with the official title once) hit all-time highs when I was struggling with my sexuality. More often than not, they weren't even official partners; just someone I happened to have given a wristy to multiple times. Being so unsure of myself, my place in the world and my relationships, I would kick the fuck off if my current fictional boyfriend mingled with another woman. I hadn't quite grasped the notion behind casual sex and found myself making solid plans for the future as I lay in the arms of a handsome stranger. If I could go back in time, I would physically shake some sense into that poor girl, and scold her for being so silly. How could you put yourself in yet another situation where inevitably you'll end up hurt? I wish I could tell her that simultaneously opening her legs and heart is a bad idea, and she'd do well to understand that sex is more natural than monogamy.

I actually think it's OK to fancy other people who

aren't your partner. Stay with me for a moment. As long as you don't fancy them instead or more than you do your own significant other, it's only human behaviour. Anyone who really knows me will vouch for the fact that I have a crush on almost everyone I meet; man, woman, non-gender conforming, cat or dog; it doesn't matter. If they are nice to look at and or charming/funny, I am all over it.

The idea of falling in love with one person and never looking at another being ever again for the duration of your life may sound drastically romantic, but we're not genetically programmed to do so. As long as you're looking and intent on not touching, there should be no real issue. My 'type on paper' (very Love Island of me) is a big old rugby player with a wealth of body hair and a passion for the sesh. And, yeah, I've basically just described my current partner. But that's not to say I don't often wake up in the mood for a skinny white boy or craving a romp with Idris Elba.

I too am aware here that I sound like some sort of man eater. But, hey, if the shoe fits.

I work with a lot of male colleagues and have a lot of guy friends; and I've fantasized about shagging just about all of them. The key thing to take note of here, is that I don't.

Admittedly, being such an incredible control freak and often overly jealous girlfriend, I adopted certain double standards. When I first met my BF, I was allowed to fancy whomever I wish, and vocalise it as and when

I saw fit, but if he even so much as double tapped his friend's latest Instagram post, all hell broke loose. Thankfully I was able to see the light in how much of an anally retentive control-witch I was and relax. A little bit, anyway. And since we've spent many a happy evening, snuggled up in bed, talking about how fit we find other people. We've even started pointing them out to each other in public. So, if he notices someone with a pulse or wearing trousers, he'll often flag them up as someone I might find aesthetically pleasing. Crucial in making this work, is always finding your partner more attractive than you find anything else (apart from yourself, of course). And, I do. Now we're four years into our relationship, I am head over heels nuts for him and his impeccable facial structure.

At this point in my life, there's lots that I've learned. Most notably, the importance of true friends and an overdraft. Well, that and the significance of having the option to enjoy casual sex. Something seldom talked about, but often considered. And given such a shitty status for never being 'enough'. Like, because you've opted for fornication without any strings attached, you are automatically deemed defective. How dull and old-fashioned. Is it scrutiny that you're bored of? Or are you bored of casual dating? Casual fucking? Are you avoiding anything that starts with 'cas' and doesn't end in 'hmere'?

As a previous successive casual shagger, allow me to give you some insight. Cosmo exposed that casual sex is proven to lead to a healthier, happier you, with 67% of women feeling noticeably more cheerful on the days they get some. I mean, it's no secret that sex releases endorphins, and who wouldn't feel elated had they woken up with some divine other nuzzled between their thighs? One night stands (as I continue to rabbit on about continuously) have a notoriously bad rep, and it's almost as if society wants to shame us into feeling guilty or sad the morning after. SAD?! After mattress mambo-ing? As long as you had healthy, consensual sex, there's really no reason to cry over spilt semen. There should be no shame in sex, and that applies to casual coitus also.

Unfortunately, casual sex/dating repeatedly with the same lucky individual is where it could get messy - both inside and outside the bedroom. Because after the first few times, the 'casual' status seems to somewhat wear off, and you find yourself asking after their Grandma and checking up on the growth of her garden tomatoes. Generally speaking, someone will develop feelings. And it's almost never both of you, so don't bank on that shit. I have lost count of the amount of times I've convinced my poor self that if I keep sucking and let him finish in my eye, that he will absolutely, definitely, no-flaws-in-this-plan fall in love with me. Never works. You just end up sore, single and partially blind. Someone will forget that the usual rules don't apply and start whatsapping their life away – flirtatious emojis and all. If you are engaging in a casual fling through genital contact, then please remember to check your emotions at the door.

On the flipside, as a singleton I often found myself growing tired of all things casual, despite my living in England's capital and dating that whole host of gentlemen for a year. Hundreds of first dates and only a handful of second dates later, and that was just it. I was bored. Living a grown up life with a big girl job, a rental and my very own Oyster card meant that casual extra-curricular activity seemed a bit out of place. I had grown up fucking around (in almost every context of the phrase), so now I was getting my shit together, surely my love life should be falling into place, too?

Perhaps I never made it past date 2 because, with all of the other first dates that I was entertaining, I wasn't applying enough attention to just one individual? Or maybe I just had one too many large vinos and exposed too much about myself. Damn. But at the end of the day, relationships won't necessarily come when you're ready for or want them. I waited two years and a whole lot more fuck buddies until I found someone worth giving up a world full of dick for. It should go without saying that involving yourself in anything labelled 'casual', will rarely get you down the aisle in the satin Vera Wang you've been lusting over.

Women are relatively simple creatures (I'm lying). And men? Oh, for crying out loud, men are even more so. Causal associations are a fun way to pass the time, providing you're both in the same boat. So, if it's an agreement that your reproductive organs are in a relationship but the remainder of your person are definitely are not, then hey, crack on. But that is nowhere near as easy as it sounds. As soon as someone starts to invest a little more emotion, then that's when you need to pull out, wipe yourself off and call it a day. Casual relationships require both a completely equal agreement and a mutual outlook on the situation, from the beginning. Providing you cause no harm to yourself or anyone else, do as you please. The truth will set you free, so ensuring you remain open and honest throughout is key.

I stand in favour of keeping it casual. It doesn't work for everyone, granted, but causal relationships can be pretty ideal. Anyone with a jam-packed diary will know that finding time for dating, let alone sex, is seldom an easy task. Often, it is situations like this that appeal most to said recipients. Women have just as many sexual needs as men and, sometimes, our battery operated buddies just won't cut it. Y'all go out and get yours, so why can't we do what we need to get ours?

Chapter 23

I've had pap smears more pleasant than some of the dates I've been on.

Prior to the slightly major high school falling out, I had dabbled in the dirty deed with a local bodybuilder. Bit of a wanker, to be honest, but the endorphins and/or performance enhancing medication may have gone to his head. I wish I could use the same excuse. We exchanged texts for about a year before he finally asked me out. Our blossoming ardor didn't last very long. He was satisfying in the sack but openly admitted to using me for my body. We had a handful of official dates, often frequenting a popular chicken restaurant. My then-foolish self used to avoid ordering chips in attempt to portray myself as super healthy, and the perfect gym-goers girlfriend. Alas, almost every time I would ended up caving and eating not only his fries, but the second portion he had to order for me.

We wound up doing that really fun thing where we engage in frequent sexual activity but only one of us is actually emotionally invested. Obviously that person was me. And obviously it was not fun. One significant sunny afternoon, he got up post-coitus to take himself home and I made the mistake of asking him for a cuddle. He politely informed me that he hadn't come over for a cuddle, and, in so many words, that I was only good for a bit of push push in the bush. He left, promptly, as I chased him down the stairs with one of my tennis shoes. It was a shit show, natural disaster style, and I cried for approximately seven months. Without having been in love with the guy, it was my first experience of heartbreak. I was just gutted to have invested so much time, energy and emotion in something with no return. I recall lying in bed and scrolling through the old texts he used to send me, wondering how cruel someone has to be to lead someone on in such a way and sniveling down the phone to my patient posse of girlfriends.

I should have learned from my mistakes. I should have avoided men who behaved like dicks just because I wanted it. But, longing for male attention of any sort, I didn't. I continued putting myself in situations where I was easily used, and winding up lonely and depressed was inescapable.

Dating isn't easy. Full stop. The 'dating game' is exactly that; a game. Trust me, I have been on enough to write them up as a goddamn movie franchise. My advice for first dates? Try and avoid telling your date that you love them. I made this mistake with my current significant other. He was making me laugh and feeding me pizza, so naturally I was confused and slightly hysterical.

Thankfully, I recovered in a very cool way, arguing as to why I did not love him, until he definitely got the message. If possible, don't drink too much champagne and burp into your date's mouth. Again, my current boyfriend was privy to this mishap on our first date. If I hadn't blown his mind with an epic shag mere hours later and been my gloriously hilarious self, I would question why he asked me out again.

Whilst on the subject of champagne, watching your alcohol intake is advisory the first time courting someone. Depending on how much you can handle, ensure you've had just enough to loosen up and converse more freely, but not so much that you find yourself singing 'should've won a Tony' show tunes to him and crying over how much you miss your ex lover's sister's dog. Basically, all you can do is turn up, be your fabulous self and hope and pray to whatever God you believe in that the person who's lucky enough to be taking you out isn't, in fact, a total and utter loon. My favourite very-bad-date story was my first and last Plenty of Fish blind date. Now, I'm all for dating apps and sites (at one point I was a member of ten, including those specialising in fantasies and much older men. Sorry, not sorry) – but you really do have to be bloody careful.

I was living in London at the time, and was desperately and un-admittedly lonely. Don't get me wrong, I had an abundance of fun-loving girlfriends and some of my favourite family members living close by, but there was seemingly something missing. Yeah, it was penis.

This particular admirer had mentioned he was a rugby playing banker, so I had obviously immediately invited him over for wine. He bought two bottles, and so we were off to an excellent start and I could drink enough to ignore the uncomfortable comments he threw into conversation about how enticing he found my body. Side note - if you're one of the very few who haven't seen my boobs before, then please be assured that they are really quite wonderful, and have served as a hot point for conversation since they first blessed me with their presence. Or just ask me the next time I'm in the pub three wines deep. I'll likely give you the live show.

The night progressed and, whilst I had already made up my mind that he was not the one for me, we had a fair amount in common and I was up to my elbows in the tortilla chips and guac that the local supermarket had so kindly provided. I was taking a short break from inhaling the crisps and dip (for both air and a sip of my pinot), when my date lunged towards me. Blissfully under the impression that he too was grabbing handfuls of snacks while he had the opportunity, I took no notice. More's the pity, the Doritos turned out not to be the object of his desire. It was I that he chose to grab instead. He took both of his rather clammy hands and slid them into each of my bra cups. Queue utter mortification and my slightly shrill demand for him to exit, immediately, and leave the wine and tortilla chips exactly where they were. I hadn't even kissed the man, and I still, to this day, haven't a clue what his last name is.

A bad date is judged that way either because of the date itself, or the actual person who you're dating. I've had pap smears more pleasant than some of the dates I've been on. And I've been on a handful of dates where the sexual attraction was absolutely there, but the chemistry just was not. And, honestly, the only thing more unsatisfactory than an Adonis with the personality of a slice of dry toast, is when the kebab shop forgets your garlic mayo. I was taken out one sunny Saturday afternoon by a chap who, no word of a lie, looked like Bradley Cooper and Dwayne Johnson's love child. Anyway, I was sipping my rosé and pretending his jokes were funny when he informed me that he didn't like Japanese food, because he couldn't use chopsticks. Naturally, I giggled away thinking that he had made another not-quite-funny joke. Turns out he was being deadly serious, and actually thought that it was against the law to eat sushi or noodles with a fork. Our riveting discussion into our favourite and least favourite cuisines continued until I let it be known that I had a strong hatred for courgettes. He thought I was talking about cars. As in a Corvette, to which he took as an incitement to ask me further and more detailed questions about exhausts and whatever else car enthusiasts talk about. Windscreen wipers, maybe. It's safe to say that we didn't make it to the second date.

I've also been on dates with great guys, in shitty settings. Its personal preference, but I really, really dislike bowling. So you can imagine how much excitement I had to fake when taken on a third date to a local alley. Bowling alley, that is, and not a damp backstreet. I don't believe in faking anything; age, orgasms or excitement. But I did it. Mostly because he liked going down on me for what seemed like hours at a time, but also because I felt a little bit guilty. He had planned a nice evening out and I wasn't about to turn around and be ungrateful. But, to me, bowling is just rent a foot disease. It's not fun and I don't like putting my fingers where other's put theirs (vaginas not included).

And, but of course, I've also experienced those great dates with great guys, only for them to decide that you are actually not that great (probs v stupid and/or high), and nothing progresses. I often daydream about the sweet April Sunday that consisted of two bottles of wine and a particular rugby player. He was pretty handsome, and his Canadian accent definitely worked in his favour. Oh, and he had the biggest hands I'd ever seen. Although not everything was in proportion, if you know what I mean. Yeah, I'm talking about his cock. Anyway, the date progressed and we went back to my place. 'My place' at the time meant the town house I shared with my mother and siblings – obviously somewhere in between the three times she kicked me out. We kissed a lot and, considering my momentous lack of self-control, I was like putty in his hands. I was adamant I didn't want to sleep with him (having learned at least something from my rugby-boning stint in London town) and so we ended up severely dry humping and with my mum returning home to me, bent over my bed, being spanked with a studded paddle through my jeans.

I dated a LOT when I lived in London. Mostly because it was expensive to socialise, and this way I was guaranteed a free meal and drinks, but also because staying in with my vibrator and a vat of frozen Bolognese sometimes got a little tedious. London is an amazing city. Alongside that, however, it really can be very lonely. I lived the life of a cosmopolitan socialite by day, but found myself tucked in with a glass of Merlot and a Calpol fast-melt come night time. And obviously by 'cosmopolitan socialite', I mean that whilst in my mind I was clip-clopping along Fenchurch Street in fabulous shoes with poise and grace, in between furious bouts of typing, reality looked a lot more like me wondering around, lost (again), lumbering through Herne Hill, slightly sticky thighs from thirty minutes on the train and out of breath from too many weekend fags, sporting the classic London working woman's look - a wrinkled dress, tights and trainers.

I lived in London for near enough a year, and there is no argument that the city is alive with excitement. Everywhere and everyone appears to be madly busy, and it truly is the city that never sleeps. You'll soon learn this if you try walking in a crowd during rush hour. Tourists moving slow enough to be lapped by a tortoise, with those trying to pass them either standing on the back of their heels or tripping over them in a bid to jump on a departing bus is like an insight into what my fiery future in Hell will be like. Sure, as a resident you soon grow tired of spending a 45 minute tube journey nestled in the crook of an elderly man's sweaty armpit, and a night out on the town costing you more than a week's rent, but there really is something wonderfully incomparable about living there.

In cities like London, you've got to take the rough with the smooth. The rough, in this sense, being squeezed onto the District Line like sardines on the one day temperatures beat 30 degrees, and wondering how on earth you didn't wind up getting off pregnant. But then all of a sudden, it's 11pm and you've miraculously made a friend with a membership to Shoreditch House, where you'll spend the evening sipping mojitos and sat next to Professor Green. Would I move back? Unlikely. I'm kind of leaning towards babies, long dog walks in empty fields and kitchen AGAs now. And not just because I'm over the city-living journalist cliché. Existing in London made me feel sophisticated and grown up - an indescribable feeling for that 19 year old small-town girl and, whilst I'm still undoubtedly a city chick, I think I'm better suited to something smaller.

I was indisputably at the height of my dating 'career' when I was London-bound. Please note, the term career here does not refer to nor mean in any way that I was an Escort, just that I spent enough time doing the damn thing that I could have made a substantial living from it, on a professional level. Dating anywhere is risky business, but in London is nothing in short of a minefield. Like with any given location, there are definitely preferably candidates in close proximity, but you really have to look to sieve them out from their wanky counterparts. Long story short, your perfect pairing definitely exists but your mission, should you choose to accept it, is to put the hours into finding them. Plus it's REALLY hard to try and find someone to actually approach you in attempt at asking you out - the majority of those living in large cities like our Nation's capital tend to be slightly unfriendly towards strangers – God forbid you look them in the eye on the tube.

WOMAN UP

Chapter 24

Romance isn't dead, it's hiding behind a smartphone.

Romance isn't dead, it's hiding behind a smartphone. With a population of over eight million people (the majority of which will probably never, ever speak to you in person) and living very much in the age of social media, can you really blame anyone for resorting to online dating? These apps or sites in any city can provide a potential partner from almost every walk of life. I'd often open my 'matches' to find my latest suitors ranged from the by day estate agent (by night, bodybuilding champion), handsome French expats, Canary Wharf suited and booted types, and someone dreadlocked and hailing from Camden way. Plus, as mentioned, I'll always have Tinder to thank for opening my eyes to the world of local premiership rugby players. Hooray for late night booty calls and secret wives they forgot to tell me about, hooray! I had the most frequent and random sexual encounters whilst living in London, and some of my best and worst ever dates (any story not detailed in these pages is probably best told over a comfortable dinner and two or three bottles of red).

Make no mistake, long gone are my days of swiping until I gave myself repetitive strain injury. But they really were the good old days, and it never hurts to ruminate. I am in full support of online dating, and it made my lonely London life a whole lot easier - that is, when I wasn't either chasing a handsome stranger out of Sloane Square tube station and wrathfully documenting his beauty on snapchat, or saving up my daily calorie allowance for numerous expresso martinis and then pouring myself over the nearest tall, dark, rugby player-resembling bloke, of course. And I seriously used to question why I was single!?

Bustling cities like London thrive on their single community. Need more proof? Find a cocktail bar with a Thursday evening happy hour (and pleeeease take me with you). Whilst I don't doubt others have a similar feel, The Big Smoke is a single girl's paradise. There are umpteen fantastic date spots, hundreds of randy bankers, gorgeous open spaces and green parks for romantic strolls. Oh, and a hotel on nearly every corner, you know, for a lunchtime quickie. You could even pull the ultimate tourist move and, after a few cocktails, rent a Boris bike for a scenic tour of the city. If, by scenic, you mean unruly pigeons chasing unsuspecting businessmen for their Pret sarnie and black cab drivers screeching around corners, hurling cockney rhyming insults at you for getting in the way.

I always recommend drinks for a first date. See prior

chapters. Most cities are bursting with micro-breweries and quirky cocktail bars and what better way to get to know someone than to spill all your secrets after half a bottle of prosecco? Again, with the not-quite-following-my-own-advice. Honestly, I really did try and limit myself to a four-drink date rule. Three if they're cocktails with more than two alcoholic ingredients. My reasoning being that that way, you tend to get a nice buzz and feel chatty enough to converse freely, without slurring your words and blabbing about the time your intimate beautician scalded your labia. Yes, I struggle with knowing my limits when it comes to party juice. So, yes, somewhere in the depths of Chiswick there is a BMW salesman who is probably scarred for life after five pornstar martinis and a graphic story telling.

The best thing about dating in London (other large-scale cities are available)? If the date goes horribly tits up or you do end up re-telling the story of when you lost your virginity in Croydon's Tesco car park, you'll probably never see them again.

I went on a date with someone in London who I'd been at school with in Scotland. He was fucking handsome, and took me out for Thai food and far too many drinks. I lived in the most beautiful riverside apartment in Battersea at the time (courtesy of my mother's very generous boyfriend) and, let me tell you, there is no way to end a date quite like being bent over a glass balcony for all passers-by on Battersea Bridge and anyone living in the same apartment block to see. Single life is oh-so-fun, but can also be massively dangerous - particularly for a woman in any large or strange city. Be careful and look after yourself, always.

Chapter 25

I recommend online dating, specifically apps, to all of my single friends.

Sometimes my friends are really great, and let me play on their Tinder profiles. I want mine back. Not because I am at all interested in meeting someone else or because I particularly want to talk to random horny blokes, but because I honestly find it so much fun. My cravings are especially high when I'm bored, hungover, or in a new place. I just want to scout some talent before running home and informing the local single community to put down their gin and tonics and follow me, pied piper style, to the city with all the handsome bachelors and bachelorettes. Although I was single (and dating) for half a decade, and never actually found this mythical place.

I feel, especially when playing via my friend's profiles, like I am some kind of superstar matchmaker and the fate of a potential relationship is in my hands. But then you swipe across someone you know has a partner or spouse, and all of a sudden everything is awkward and no one is looking each other in the eye.

People most commonly use dating sites to meet someone that they can date and/or shag. It's a tool for flirting. It's not just to see hot, naked singletons – they would surely opt for porn if all they were after was a close-up vagina shot (well, that or my personal picture archive). Dating sites are predominantly a hunting tool to bag someone that you hope to eventually slip into bed, and potentially something more long term, with. And there is just no shame in that. The evenings of those single years were spent glued to my mobile, forever holding a glimmer of hope that my dream man was out there, within 40km of me and between the ages of 22 and 40. Plus, I enjoyed the compliments and cheesy chat up lines.

I recommend online dating, specifically apps, to all of my single friends. The optimum word here being 'single'. The world of e-dating is not somewhere you take yourself when you've had a row with your partner or have decided that being with one person for the rest of your days is no longer an option. I mean it is, of course, providing you've let that partner know beforehand. When a person makes a relationship milestone, logically, they are going to wonder whether or not this is the last sexual partner they'll have and contemplate if others would still deem them shaggable should the relationship not work out. The urge to cheat is natural – I get that. As humans, we are not designed to mate for life. But this doesn't mean that infidelity is forgivable. Imagine this scenario - You meet him or her online. You fall in love online. You then take your profiles down together to live your happy offline life. The End. Or is it?

I've known of long term couples discovering their partner on various online dating services. Sometimes, this comes after their relationship hit a rocky patch. It was by no means over, but definitely sealed the deal in the final stages of their romance. But, sometimes, this comes as a surprise and is completely out of the blue. If you are interested in what else is out there, and are losing interest in your current companion - just bite the fucking bullet and break up with them. It's unfair if you don't, and you'll come off as a much worse person for stringing them along. You end up wasting everyone's time and earning yourself a less than ideal reputation. So save us all the hassle, and act like a grown up. It's hard to lay blanket rules down as every couple and relationship are obviously very different, but there's one thing I know for sure.

If I caught my boyfriend/fiancé/husband, online or otherwise, flirting with someone else, I couldn't and wouldn't stand for it. I have enough respect for myself to know I deserve more respect than that. He would be out on his arse and I would be taking full custody of any shared assets of value. I imagine that most grown up couples actually have these in the form of property, furniture, cars etc, and not just a freezer drawer full of gourmet fish fingers and imported Scotch pies.

If you are doing something behind your significant

other's back, and the thought of them uncovering the truth panics you, then you've given some sort of false impression of yourself and you are doing something wrong. Perhaps you're innocent and naïve (or bored on a Thursday evening, like me), and are creating a profile on Hinge or Tinder just to see what's out there – and, hey, if your partner is OK with that, then you go right ahead and swipe. But if you are sneaking around behind their back and are popping off for a poo every half an hour to check your likes - take a deep breath, sit back and re-evaluate your relationship.

I reckon that online flirting is considerably worse than a drunken snog with a local bartender on a night out. And here's why. Online flirting and sexting is cold, sober and intentional. You have your full wits about you and you are actively seeking someone to flirt with – regardless of whether or not your intentions include meeting said person. I know both men and women who've created secret profiles or reactivated their previous profiles temporarily after a bump in the road in their relationships, just to have a gander at what is out there. Not cool, guys. Not cool at all.

While this is relatively common, it's also incredibly hurtful. As big as the digital dating horizon is, there are too many friends and family members who will almost definitely see your profile, even if it's only up for a few days or so. They show your mutual friends. They show a big ass picture of you, and as long as you're within 40km (insert preferred distance here), you'll be busted, it will blow up, and that might not be recoverable - so is it worth the risk? Are you on Tinder for a quick gander, or for a flirt? Are you nosy, or unhappy?

At the end of the day, cheating is cheating. Whether you're physically cheating or emotionally cheating, and whether it's porking your secretary or hiding behind a profile that advertises you as a 6ft4 cage fighting champion - you're being unfaithful. Just consider next time you need an ego-boost quick fix and you reach for your smart phone; is it worth losing someone important over? If yes, please see all helpful advice mentioned above and cut all ties with your poor, poor other half.

WOMAN UP

Chapter 26

Like most other unruly wild women, such behaviour made its debut in my younger years.

From what you've already read, I'm almost certain that you'll have come to terms with the fact that I was not a well behaved child. Like most other unruly wild women, such behaviour made its debut in my younger years. Not thrilled with the birth of my sister and inevitable sharing of my parent's undivided attention, I frequently used to bite her and run for the hills, or pick moments when my mother was rendered useless (for example, with a baby clamped to her tit), and scale the fireguard before knocking everything in reach off the mantelpiece.

My first experience socialising with children other than my now painfully annoying two year old sister, was at nursery, where I met some of my best friends to date. As was normal for me at this point, I was full of sass, determination and inquisitiveness. Basically, I was a tiny dictator looking to build an army out of her fellow snotty playmates. My recruitment process went a little something like this – picture me, exactly the same but some five feet shorter, curly hair and a big mouth, stomping around the playground in lace up boots and no trousers, demanding everyone befriend me. After this *bizarrely* didn't pan out, I found a friend in one of the quieter girls. I invited her into my coveted circle and, as part of her initiation, demanded she try and eat a red plastic tea pot. She gave it her best go, and we became inseparable. Some years later, after a falling out over a back garden picnic nightmare, I locked her in my room, barricaded the door with my doll's changing table and, quite seriously, threatened to kill her if she tried to escape. She ended up crying for help from my bedroom window and I ended up grounded for the rest of the holidays. It's a true miracle that we are still so close now.

At around eight, and having learned the true power behind swear words, I often found myself flipping the bird at anyone who dared cross me (40 year old neighbours included) before speeding off on my neon mountain bike as fast as my stumpy little legs could pedal. Obviously, between 15-20 minutes later, I would then be summoned in by my mother for the pending scold that awaited me.

Succeeding the virginity attempt and swift move down to England was when I became somewhat obsessed with male attention. It wasn't something I had experienced in great detail prior, and having been essentially boarded up in a same sex school, I was getting none of it. I retorted back to the less than charming youths and less than favourable reputation from my last place of education, and gifted them with the abundance of naked selfies I took on a daily basis. And I took loads. And they loved it – why wouldn't they, I was desperately seeking attention and living off their every word and demand as a result. I couldn't have been more physically virginal, and yet found myself sexting like my school dinner depended on it. It became somewhat of a downward spiral, and the situation I had put myself in landed me in quite a bit of trouble. Initially, my parents found my phone and camera and all of the illicit content they contained. This was bad enough, and resulted in me losing my phone, on several occasions, for months at a time. I didn't have an actual real life camera phone until I was nineteen. No joke.

And yes, I thought that my parents seeing the pictures and videos of my *very* naked body was the worst that could happen. But boy, was I wrong. The only part of this that I am to blame for, is trusting those who should not have been trusted. I was completely naïve and technically still a child, so had no prior warning not to trust the various boys who became the lucky inheritors of my cyber sex. Those who were lucky enough to be on the receiving end actually turned out to be mean and immature boys, who inevitably sent my precious pictures to just about everyone they came into contact with. They printed copies and stapled them to the lunchroom walls at the school I had not long since left. They posted them on Facebook and only agreed to delete them after hours spent tearfully begging.

Before you tell me that I shouldn't have distributed

nudes if I didn't want them seen by the world, think about the bigger picture. Nobody tells victims of muggings that they could have avoided it by staying home always. Revenge porn is real life, and it's really fucking illegal. It is the sharing of nudes that is shameful, not the taking of them.

After the nightmare of having all of my friends see all of me, it emerged that, not only did they publish them for every member of my hometown to see, but they were also shared illegally on various popular photo sharing sites, along with a link to my Facebook page. Not quite how I'd imagined my first fifteen minutes of fame, I'll tell you that for free.

For weeks I had strangers messaging me and telling me they'd seen me on this site. Please take a minute at this point to imagine my poor, poor IT teacher, who, after asking me what said pictures were of (I contacted him for advice about how to get the pictures offline, as it were), was met with the response 'of me fingering my hoop, Sir'. He swiftly excused himself and never really looked at me again. Not only was it revenge porn, but also sexual harassment and, considering my age at the time of distribution, child porn. The pictures circulated various countries, including Japan, Australia and Germany – where someone sent the link to one of their friends, who just happened to work for my Dad. Yep, my dad had now also been sent the link. Oh, the shame. Thankfully, he knew that I would never have widely shared such intimate images myself, and was more concerned with those distributing and downloading pictures of a fifteen year old girl.

I learned from my mistakes. I never stopped taking and sending pictures of myself, I just made sure that at least something was left to the imagination and I became incredibly conscious of what I was putting out and onto the World Wide Web. As in, I no longer took close up clit shots or those of my bum hole. Self-timer really is a wonderful thing. In fact, I learned to love my nudes. And, when predictably they were sent round again (different pictures, different crowds, different occasions), I offered an autograph to anyone who mentioned them to me and even made them into a handy little video so people could keep them all in one place. I was in my late teens, and I knew I looked good – so, why not? If you've got it, flaunt it.

Technically, I'm no longer a child. And despite my frequent tantrums and the resting sulk face I've been wearing since age 5, I'm approaching my late-twenties. But I don't feel like a grown up. Sure, I live with another almost grown up human being, and we pay rent and talk about babies and not being able to afford wine that doesn't come in a screw top bottle, but I'm not ready to grow up yet - and don't judge me for it. I spend a fair portion of my life thinking about, reminiscing over and laughing about carefree summers. In particular, the summers of 2013 and 2014 seem to have been the making of me. Sounds a little corny, but do come along on this little trip down memory lane with me. That is, Memory Lane, San Antonio, Ibiza.

In 2014, we visited the White isle. This is that first

and last girl's holiday I was telling you about earlier. Call me shallow, but nothing makes me happier than the memory of eight naked girlfriends, lying around a pool, doubled over with laughter before staggering into the closest tattoo parlour to brand our vaginas with a love heart. Trust me, nothing screams true love like having it permanently etched on your bits. The majority of us were single, still living at home and doing whatever we wanted – life was a simple thing. Little did I know, it was the last hoorah for the crazy, drunk friends I so loved to party with.

Chapter 27

Your friends are the most important people in your life. They are the family that we choose for ourselves.

I know I've only just reached my mid-twenties, but with best friends three and four years my senior and a boyfriend a few years older than them, I am old before my time. By the time this book finally gets published, I have no doubt that some of my nearest and dearest will be married, some will have babies and some will be flying high career-wise. We are forced, as teens and young adults, to make massive decisions regarding our career path, future and the rest of our lives – and I'm sure I'm not alone in wishing I was still carefree, pissed out my nut and naked as a babe.

Over the last seven years, I've fallen in love with my friends. Who else can you go out with, for the sole reason of toasting their new pair of tits? And for that reason, I would never even consider finding new, younger friends to re-live the last few years with (as people have suggested). Finding people that you connect with in the way that my friends and I do is extremely rare, and I've never come across a group of girls quite like us. This is why I want to grow up with them. Regardless of the (tiny, if you really look at it) age gap, I want to get married at the same time as they do, have babies at the same time as them (a miniature gang - how cute) and grow old with them. We support each other in so much; it would be really unfortunate for us not to carry that on for the rest of our lives.

Don't get me wrong, sometimes, I can't wait to grow up. My friends have bought houses, birthed children, have pets of their own, live in entirely different countries and have the type of really grown up jobs that change people's lives. Being around all this inspiration, it's only natural that I'd want the same. I want to get married, and have thousands of babies - I often frighten my boyfriend off with how much planning I've actually done, but at the same time; I long to be carefree and 18 again. At the time, I hated it. I wished myself older so I could be more like my new and older friends. Not to run the risk of sounding like the reincarnation of your Great Aunt Maud, but enjoy your youth while you can.

I spent the summer before my 19th birthday in a state described only as 'permanently blootered', through weeknight visits to our local pub, liquid lunches and waiting all week for Friday, to begin yet another weekend of hilarious drunk, naked, careless fun. That summer, I think I smiled for three months straight - and this was all before the chapter of boyfriends, mortgages and saving.

Don't get me wrong, our lives now are amazing, and I

wouldn't want to change that. We are who we are because of those wonderful years and let me tell you something, swapping out all night benders for dancing at your best friend's wedding is more amazing than I'd ever have given it credit for.

As mentioned, my best friends are in their late twenties (and will likely kill me for mentioning it), and I am a couple of years their junior. When the girls were celebrating their 21st birthdays (it genuinely feels like this was two months ago), we had just met and were about to embark on what would quite literally be the time of our lives. Now, they are mature and fantastic, and I am beyond proud of them, but I'm sort of stuck at square one, in between staying up all night and making a tit of myself and swapping painting the town red for a pizza and a film with my other half. I don't feel like I missed out on my youth; I am fairly confident that I've done everything that I would have having had younger friends, but I don't doubt that I wished some of it away, desperate to prove to everyone how mature I had become. Rest assured, this was after I was found naked and in the starfish position, on some random Spanish balcony, snuggled up to half a kebab.

You know when you look back at old pictures of yourself and find yourself baffled at how carefree you were (after spending your days whining about being stressed) and how simpler times were back then? Boy oh boy, nothing puts your life into perspective quite like remembering how chilled you used to be. I know, I know, missing that bus and turning up to the party when everyone else was two WKDs in was suuuch a big deal. And your good jeans being in the wash was practically life ruining. I had no cares. And, don't get me wrong, I'm pretty easy going now, but alongside that, I also have a job to keep, rent to pay and a live-in boyfriend to feed. But I have happy and hilarious memories of, the morning after a night out, emptying my clutch bag with my girlfriend and being unbelievably thrilled that we could total up our coppers and leftover jagerbomb change to make £11. Back then, that was enough for 10 cigarettes and a double cheeseburger each. That Sunday afternoon, we felt like we were living like royalty.

I do try and live in the moment as much as possible. And, now we're that bit older and ever so slightly more serious, it's become easier to lead - some of my friends in particular – astray in convincing them to re-live their party years and join me in recalling on those times until the wee hours. But, I do often subconsciously find myself behaving not dissimilarly to my Gran. My cousin and I habitually do a crossword together via WhatsApp, and I've been known to leave a cocktail party early in order to get home in time for my grocery delivery. For me, happy hour is slowly becoming getting into bed at 9pm on a Friday and settling down to Netflix and wine in my comfiest pyjamas. I mean, come on - I'm not even trying to cling on to my youth! It often seems as though I've traded in my heels and vodka for a warm cardigan and a Zimmer frame.

Despite my perpetual moaning, I wouldn't change the last half a decade for anything. Obviously, there have been some truly awful times, but I'd be afraid that if I ever went back, I'd somehow do something different and the memory as a whole would be ruined. I am easing myself into being ready to let go of my crazy and slightly inappropriate partying years, knowing that there are so many other adventures I am going to embark on both alone and with my posse of powerful women – they just might not necessarily include illegal drugs or copious amounts of alcohol, so stay tuned.

If I could give today's younger generation any advice, (obviously other than warning them against hard core substances and poisonous boyfriends), it would be to embrace every single moment, even the ones that you think are really shit and dead boring because you don't have enough money to buy pre-drinks or a new top. Because (and I really sound like my mother now) before you know it, it will all be a fond but distant memory.

Your friends are the most important people in your life. They are the family that we choose for ourselves, and they've got a pretty good chance of outliving your spouse. I am (boring you with the same story) so eternally grateful for my friends. I have grown up going to various different schools and have had various different friendship groups. You learn who your true friends are by realising who's there for you and who isn't and learning to let them go. As well as a handful of childhood friends who I will keep clutched to me forever, I can now officially say that my current gaggle, as well as being my saving grace, are my homies for life. Particularly because I'm unsure if I'll ever find another assembly of women willing to put up with my relentless nudity/crazy ideas/passion for doner meat. Hand on heart; if I hadn't fallen into my current friendship group then my life would be unimaginably different.

Chapter 28

Not all little girls daydream about being princesses.

I've had a multitude of 'careers'. A real abundance of odd jobs. I've done sales and marketing and telesales and been the person you call when your Mars bar doesn't taste right. I've sold cars and tills and worked with cranes and, honestly, it's all bollocks. I met some great people along the way, but wasting your time doing something you don't want to do is as pointless as the work you will produce. Don't stick at a job which makes you miserable - I did, and I wound up the most miserable and bitter singleton in central London. I should never have stayed in school for as long as I did; it was pointless me being there for the 2 hours a week that I could roll myself out of bed for to get less than desirable A Level results. Discover your talents and find your passion. If I hadn't sworn myself off men and documented every last detail, you wouldn't be sat here reading this book.

Again, I'm trying really hard not to complain. Sure, retirement is looking pretty good right now but, short of counting down the next 40-odd-years, sometimes you've just gotta sell a little bit of your soul and do what you can to put baked beans on the table. I believe in everything happening for a reason. I was obviously meant to work in the fiery pits of hell so I could leave and pursue other things. But don't let the fact that I've had more jobs than checkups with the gynaecologist be what you take away from this. The takeaway is to keep dreaming.

Not all little girls daydream about being princesses. That might sound stereotypical, but I hope you'd be surprised at how often I hear it. When adults talk to children, especially girls, they can often be heard telling them how pretty they are, and how much like a princess/fairy/angel they look. They are given dolls and prams and Barbies to dress up. All the while, their brothers are described as 'heartbreakers' even before they can speak. Gross. They are encouraged to play with guns and trucks and are laughed at if seen wearing a dress or playing daddy. What are you afraid of – your son growing up to be a good father? It is unhealthy to force gender norms onto anyone; let alone those of such a young age. When painting her own nails, my mum used to do ours too, which includes me, my sister and my brother.

I never wanted to be a princess. My first sought after profession was actually to be a monk. I quite fancied the quiet life and I knew that wearing a robe and I was pretty damn sure I had the bone structure to rock a buzz cut. In turn, I was somewhat distraught when I learnt that it's almost always a male-oriented profession.

The goddamn Patriarchy ruins the party again. I then decided that a nun was the next best thing. I had watched Fräulein Maria parading around Austria countless times and was almost certain that I could learn to make play clothes from old drapes. Plus, although I couldn't match any of the talent in *Sister Act*, their lives seemed far from boring. This particular fantasy lasted until I learned that nuns couldn't get married. And until I took Textiles for GCSE, and ended up fabric gluing everything together following the revelation that, actually, I couldn't sew for shit. I then set my heart on being a big time magazine editor. I already had 'team management' (AKA, bossing my siblings, parents and friends around) down to a tee. I had obviously preempted my unwillingness to work under anyone else, too. For years I pretended that I was the next Miranda Priestly, destined to run my own successful fashion magazine. My life goals now are similar, although its women and women's rights that I want to write about.

I decided, at fifteen, that my career path should follow that of a porn star and, when asked during assembly, I had no qualms in explaining this to my gob-smacked peers and disapproving teaching staff. The moral of this story isn't to encourage your children to pursue a career in pornography or elope to a convent. But, who gives a damn if they do. Let people be who they want and pick out their own paths; and this applies to both future jobs and children's toys.

Tell everyone you know that it's OK to dream. We

should feel encouraged to fight for our dreams and to always have the highest aspirations for ourselves. I have known that writing is my dream for some time now - and I have been fighting for it since. For the past five years, I have poured my heart and soul into building a career in journalism. I quit a bloody good job and went freelance for 18 months. And, for anyone out there not associated with writing, 'freelancing' loosely translates to working your arse off in the most bizarre routine (because good ideas only come at 03:00am, and not in between the hours of 09:00am – 17:00pm like you'd hope they would) for little to no financial return. I love writing, and I would never give it up; not for love, money or chicken nuggets. It is my passion and, despite the odd mental breakdown cured only by a three hour bath and two bottles of Malbec, I am determined to pursue a career in something that I feel so strongly towards.

Your back up is key when striving for something difficult. And I don't mean hard drives and paper copies, I mean those who look out for you and back you up at every conceivable occasion. Instead of being told I was foolish to quit my job without knowing where my next paycheck was coming from, I should have been told I was brave. Instead of being pushed into 'time passing' jobs that I had categorically no interest in, I should have been supported whilst working through whatever rut I was stuck in at the time. The universe is full of quotes and sayings encouraging us to strive for the best and never stop believing in ourselves. It's all well and good being told to follow your dreams – but we need to be told how really fucking difficult it is.

It is often discussed that achieving one's goals will result in joy, personal satisfaction and an overwhelming sense of accomplishment. I have felt like a failure at least once a week ever since I embarked on this journey. I have had moments of sheer frustration that I still haven't made it. But, an early night and a good idea later, I re-assess the situation and remember that I will.

Millennials, in particular, are heralded to seize the moment, quit that financially stable but hated job and sprint toward 'the dream'. The expectation is that, the moment you make the change and follow your heart, you'll automatically find happiness you never felt before. And, sure, for the first few weeks of 'freedom' you'll be upbeat, motivated and ambitious. But prepare yourself for the unhappiness, laziness and sudden-death feeling that you're not only un-employed but also on the brink of depression that inevitably follows. This is a terrifyingly real threat and, in this moment, it's all too easy to lose your way and fall into the downward spiral.

The truth is, no matter which career path you take – stress and unhappiness, in one form or another, are unavoidable. Just because you finally decided to go for your goal, doesn't mean it will be rainbows and sparkles at the other end. It'll be just as stressful, disheartening and shitty as your previous, lacklustre job – but with one major difference; it's your dream and you have worked to be there. They don't call it work for nothing, honey.

It's not supposed to be a walk in the park. Sort of like a blowjob being given said name as a result of it being actually quite tedious and not entirely fulfilling.

My first public article, published anywhere other than my blog, came over a year after I started sending copies of my work to various magazines and websites. I wrote about anything and everything I could think of and sent it to anyone with an accessible email address. It was not easy. I was rejected more times than I had ever deemed possible. But this journey isn't about deciding what you want to do, applying for and instantaneously landing your dream job. It is getting up after you've been knocked down, rejected and criticised for the first, second and 45th time. It is perseverance and clear vision, and never losing sight of your end goal. Things worth having are worth fighting for; they aren't meant to fall straight into your lap.

Do not take this as discouragement; you can do whatever you set your mind to – but don't expect it to come easy. And don't compare yourself to the incomparable. Top tip – in the real world, Carrie Bradshaw would never have been able to afford a New York Brownstone and an abundance of Manolos on a weekly columnist's salary. Oh, and she definitely wouldn't have been able to afford to eat out at all the hottest restaurants for lunch and dinner daily.

I started my blog, The Man Ban, one late September Monday. I had just turned 20, and was living in London. The weekend prior, I had been out celebrating my birthday with my very best girls in my very favourite gay bars. Unfortunately, the night ended on a sour note and I fell asleep cuddled up to my gal pals, sobbing over a boy. In retrospect, I was arguably emotionally wobbly anyway, after a gay man in one of Soho's hottest locations refused to snog me. He had politely informed me that he wasn't into fanny, but I was the birthday girl and wearing a tiara, for Christ's sake. Anyway, we went home and I went on to drunk dial my then love interest.

Throughout my blog, he was referred to as 'The Bearded Man', and he was effing wonderful. We never actually met (he wasn't the first or last of my cyber romances), but spoke on the phone, Facetime and almost every other method of communication daily for a good few months. And I did fall for him a little. I honestly can't stop myself. I fall sooooo quickly. A compliment and/or a cheeky smile and I've tripped and fallen head over heels. But I was smitten. He was easy on the eyes and we used to send each other voice notes of our renditions of popular musical anthems so, naturally, I had deemed him perfect. Obviously I was wrong and my birthday celebrations came crashing down when he picked up the phone at 5am, only to tell me he'd started seeing someone else and promptly hung up. I've told you I don't cope with emotion overload well, and I spent the next few hours and most of the following day naked, wrapped in a cashmere blanket now ruined with mascara tears, inconsolably sobbing to my friends in between mouthfuls of Dominos.

Is it possible to fall in love with someone you've never met? I'm not suggesting this was the case, despite how insistent I was at the time. But, can you? Surely regular Skype sessions are almost the same as regular dates? I'm not convinced either way. Without boning, there's probably only so much bodily contact and language that bridges the gap between virtual and real life dates. And if you've ever watched *Catfish*, you can back me up here. These people talk for months and even years, and spark fully fledged relationships without seeing each other in any way other than on a screen. And, obviously, before they discover that their partner is actually 43 years older than originally advertised.

Whilst to this day, I'm still totally mad at him for ruining my birthday night and never granting me the closure I really needed so as not to pine after him for the coming months, I really ought to thank him for being the reason behind my blog. It took that bout of rejection for me to finally sit back and realise that, for the previous four years, my life had revolved around men and where my next love interest was coming from. If I wasn't already spending my days whatsapping at least one male suitor, I was swiping through Tinder and Facebook at a steady pace in order to find myself someone new. I just didn't know how to live my life without the presence of a boy. And so, I swore myself off the he-devils and I started a blog as a diary entry to track my progress. The rest was history. The blog became popular, and I kept writing it once I'd gone back to the D. Eventually, it lead to the launch of my website, social channels and freelance journalism career. Oh, and this bloody book. Thanks, bearded man. If I ever see you again (or full stop), I'll buy you a whisky.

WOMAN UP

Chapter 29

These were not Project X style house parties. There were no disco lights and red plastic cups, and the only topless drunk girl was me.

My verging-on-dangerous obsession with aforementioned particular sportsmen wasn't my only downfall. Having 'grown apart' from my high school girlfriends and fallen into cahoots with my local lover, so began a whole new friendship group. Friday evenings became a strict routine – finishing school (on the very few days that I actually attended), heading home for a bath and a glass of cheap rose, and dolling myself up before heading to the local. It was different in the days of yore – every second person you ran into you'd either dated/slept with/been to school with/bought a Sambuca for last Christmas Eve. It was fun, and meant that I could go out on my own and wind up spending the night with great friends. And, in their defence, they were great friends. The twenty-something group of boys who became my favourites looked after me. Some were brothers of my now best friends, and I have them to thank for introducing us. But there was one somewhat adverse habit that united us all.

In all honesty, when I talk and think about taking drugs now, it makes me feel super anxious and gives me all the butterflies. But back then was a whole different story. There was no anxiety and no little winged insects – just 9am bed times and dealer boyfriends. I actually really liked him. And I'm *fairly* sure it wasn't just the free gear. He was sweet, and I was young and easily influenced. Nevertheless, it was a short-lived fling. It came to an eventual end when he took me out for an evening of dogging. Romantic, right? It turns out his pre-planning wasn't quite adequate, and we ended up parked in front of the gate to a large livestock field. This only became an issue once the farmer realised he didn't have access, and so poked his head into the ajar window, much to my sheer horror as I lay, naked and sweaty, folded up like a human pretzel in the backseat of his Volkswagen Golf.

Regardless of my on and off fella, my friendship with his group of friends continued to blossom. I was living with my dad having been kicked out by my mother for the second time, and he was almost never around. I was in my element and most weekends had 'house parties'. Now don't be fooled, these were not *Project X* style house parties. There were no disco lights and red plastic cups, and the only topless drunk girl was me. They were more a gathering of similarly high individuals, sat around the dining room table chain smoking and draining the alcohol cupboard (sorry again, Dad).

Considering the frequency at which these events happened, it's a miracle that I can differentiate between them. But, for some reason, I can't seem to get out of my head the image of five of us, having locked ourselves in my upstairs bathroom, inhaling substances like they were going out of fashion and giving each other massages. Mere hours later, I went on to have a bath. With the room full of people and the bath sides covered in suspicious white powder.

My scandalous affair with narcotics came to an abrupt end after consuming something. I can only call it something as, to this day, I have no fecking idea what it was. But, it tipped me wayyyyy over the edge and I ended up locked in a pub toilet, smashing glasses all over myself in a vague attempt to stand up and take myself home. I failed, and ended up being carried out of the pub by the manager, following him breaking down the door to free me after an hour of panic and several contemplations of spending the night snuggled up to the toilet bowl. Fresh air contributed to sobering me up, and I went home. Not to my home, like a sensible girl would do, but to my close friend's home, where this week's after party was being held.

Knowing that at this point I couldn't ingest anything nasally (and I said I wasn't sensible), I opted to do so orally. Again, I completely oppose regrets, but if there were ever something to look back on with remorse – this was it. I woke up with the webbed skin below my tongue completely ulcered and pretty much dissolved. It was just as disgusting as you can imagine, and that combined with not being able to talk properly for almost a fortnight put me off anything 'Class A' for a really long time.

My mum thinks my slight addiction was a result of my processing her and my dad's divorce. They surprised my siblings and I with a separation in 2012. I was 17 and honestly, didn't make that much of it. Obviously, my brother and sister were 10 and 15 respectively and weren't so chill. But consciously, I just didn't mind. I love my mum and I love my dad and, although at varying points in my life I've had almighty rows with both of them, I want them to be happy. And they are, now they're officially divorced and with their new partners.

Whilst on the subject of marriage and the dissolution of, partnering for life has never really been my bag. You know I think 'The One' is bollocks. You have the ability to change so much as a person, that for one person to change with you in the necessary ways is so difficult, and is why relationships take so much work. It's cool if your relationship doesn't work out. Obviously it's shitty for a while, but inevitably it will lead to something better, contribute to your being, and for crying out loud it doesn't mean you never loved them! I'm approaching my mid-twenties and I know I've already been in love twice. And I'm here for it.

Chapter 30

Hell hath no fury like a woman scorned.

I have a very addictive personality. So it wasn't surprising when my love for hallucinogens was discovered. I have and remain to be addicted to men. This addiction presents itself in classic needy wifey. I think it's cute. Neediness is so often frowned upon, but you know you'd complain if you didn't have someone pandering after you. But nooooo, God forbid we radiate affection and express a desire to be with you. Instead, we are more often than not just labelled negatively. It's high time we stopped using 'crazy' and 'psycho' as descriptive insults.

Sure, I have behaved questionably in my time, perhaps warranting mental health inspection, but I am getting pretty pissed off watching helpless women tagged with such a description for doing nothing. 'Crazy' and 'psycho' are just convenient words used by critics to authorise their superiority. How many times have you and your friends sat around scrutinising every incoming crush-sent text and over-analysing your replies just in case you come across clingy or crazy? We are deemed mentally unstable when we do anything that makes - more often than not a man - feel remotely uncomfortable.

A friend of mine and his fiancé are infamous for arguing a lot. Whereas, in actual fact, they argue no more than the rest of us. The only difference is that this poor girl's boyfriend runs off post-row and bitches to all of his friends about how much of a nutter the woman he's engaged to is. Is she really in the wrong for fighting her corner and not letting her other half get away with behaving badly? Or just speaking her mind and voicing her opinions? Would you stand for that? Sometimes the expressing of emotions isn't pretty. Sometimes it will make others feel uncomfortable – but no healthy relationship comes from lack of acknowledging and expressing feelings.

We aren't crazy for sticking up for ourselves.

Dismissing female emotion as 'crazy' isn't something millennials have come up with. 'Female Hysteria' was a genuine medical diagnosis for centuries – most widely diagnosed in the Victorian era. To justify such verdict, a woman would show signs of anxiety, irritability, increased or decreased libido and insomnia. Let us now form a prayer circle, thanking the good lord above that we can't be committed through sex drive and/or anxiety today.

Women are more in touch with their emotions than

men; it's been scientifically proven. So how come when a man displays a classic 'crazy woman' reaction – shouting/screaming/smashing china in sheer frustration – it just isn't spoken about. Just how often do you hear about the 'psycho boyfriend'? It is pinned on women because as the 'more emotional' sex we are an easier target. Should a woman pursue a guy who has expressed disinterest? Crazy! But a man who behaves in the same way? Cute and endearing. Women speaking their feelings are met with 'You're overreacting' and 'Don't be so sensitive'. Any woman in said situation would be described as emotional, whilst a man would be deemed logical.

Tell me - what would you rather? That your girlfriend spoke out when she had a problem with something or felt uncomfortable? Or that she bitched about it for the majority of that week on her girl's WhatsApp group? I understand that women may merit the word 'psycho' through especially bad behaviour such as murder etc etc, but there's nothing wrong with women fighting for what they believe in – for example, their boyfriend sleeping with someone else. Ah the classic psycho ex, kicking off because she found out you cheated on her. What a fucking crazy bitch, right? OR, maybe, someone who's not only heartbroken, but now frustrated, angry and totally confused about the relationship she's just left. Hell hath no fury like a woman scorned.

I shouldn't be punished for ensuring my boyfriend knows when he's in the wrong and when I'm pissed off. Upon googling 'psycho girlfriend' you are greeted with copious articles (and I'm talking thousands) about how to tell if you're dating one, or, even better; how to stop yourself being one. In short, society wants us to sit pretty, ignoring our partner's ignorance and bad behaviour and letting them do whatever they want. Almost definitely contributing to the reason why so many women avoid speaking out, standing up for themselves, and even reporting assaultive behaviour to the authorities.

Once you've been in a serious relationship with a partner, it isn't natural to be able to let them go like a fart in the wind. There are going to be tears, accidental liking of Instagram posts, and tequila-fuelled angry voicemails. The sole reason you hear more about this behaviour coming from women as opposed to their male counterparts is because women tend not to keep their feelings shut off from the world, actually speak out about their problems, let it be known when they are upset and seek advice for all of the above. From personal experience, men tend to lean towards the 'ignoring that anything every happened and all parties involved' theory. Yes, there are times when women need to keep their emotions in check, but it is ridiculous and unfair that our expressing of emotions implies that we are unhealthy.

Lest we forget that using terms such as 'crazy', 'psycho' and 'bipolar' in describing anyone is disrespectful to mental illness and those who suffer with it. Merely using these words in an insulting way encourages a lot of stereotypes that discourage people from seeking out mental health help when they need it. Stigmatizing mental illness is a big problem in our society — so let's not perpetuate it by throwing these adjectives around as an insult.

WOMAN UP

Chapter 31

It is the presence or absence of a vibrating friend that completes the woman.

My taste in men would be described as questionable – and I know this is the calling card for almost every other penis inclined singleton. I spent so long dreaming about what it would be like to have a boyfriend and wake up to breakfast in bed and a morning shag (little did I know), that there honestly wasn't time for me to meet someone naturally. I have been on more dates in those five active years than my mother went on in her entire life – post divorce and all. After all, I am the only hell my mother ever raised.

I never used to decline the offer of a date. Whilst the free food and drink was often a persuasion factor, this was more down to my sheer desperation for love and attention. I went out with colleagues, friends of friends and even blokes that I met in the queue at the chippy (it's no wonder I barely got any A Levels). And, when I'd just about cleared the town of eligible (and not so) bachelors, I decided to ditch the dick. My lesbian love life was short lived, but not without excitement. She was a Playboy model and a BabeStation star, and the perfect partner to partake in a fanny fling with. Raise your hand if you've got an erection.

Full disclosure - it wasn't my first girl-on-girl rodeo. Without being a complete cliché, I did a little experimenting in my single sex school days. But I was fifteen and it was mostly just snogging practise, with a bit of fumbling. Although I could swear someone grabbed my left tit one evening when I was asleep in the boarding house. And that's not even the good one. We had no male attention, and only each other to entertain ourselves. We spent a lot of time in swimsuits and learnt how to perfectly execute a group spooning session. These were the girls that I first got drunk with, got high with and tried smoking with. We would spend evenings trying out various make up tricks and bizarre sexual positions that we found online. One of my best friends was Japanese, and used to return from home with her arms brimming with delicious snacks, Hello Kitty notebooks and my very first dildo. I have a lot to thank her for.

So, I dated a woman. And it was amazing. Just like every other date in the sense that we both had a fair few cocktails, and found ourselves subconsciously caressing each other's legs, but new and exciting in the fact that we were on similar emotional levels. It was like a dream come true – almost as if I had the perfect combination between best friend and boyfriend. We were able to talk honestly about our lives and feelings and no one was bragging about their new car or their best mate who may or may not have shagged Cat Deeley.

If it wasn't for my sudden spell of panic, I'm confident we would have progressed further. But it was the bus stop ear-whispering that made my mind up. She was very polite in her description of exactly what she wanted to do to both me and my nether regions, but for me, it only cemented the fact that I'm just not gay. I absolutely love women, often spend hours fawning over them on Social Media and can appreciate any and all beauty, but I'm not a lesbian. I watch a shit tonne of lesbian porn, and would without a doubt partake in a threesome with a partner of each sex. I actually prefer women to men. I prefer their company, the way they look and, the way they are much better at connecting emotionally. But I just can't live a life without willy. Sorry, not sorry. This truly is proof that sexuality is not a choice.

My mum found my gorgeous dildo in my bedside drawer. It was a flouro pink rampant rabbit, with a face. And I loved it. I used to excuse myself from dinner and take myself upstairs for what I accurately grew to describe as 'me time'. Basically, I'd nip upstairs and masturbate senselessly. I remember my first orgasm to this day… I felt bizarrely warm from the inside out, and like my legs were going to cramp up and never straighten again. It was a lightheaded blur of pure passion, and I actually had to google it afterwards to make double sure that it was an orgasm that I'd had, and not a mini stroke.

This was the very beginning of my love of sex toys. When starting my blog and swearing myself off men in 2014, one of my gorgeous gal pals gifted me with a medium sized vibrator which I affectionately named BOB (battery operated boyfriend). He is still with me to this day. I did have a minor break down though, when after a weekend trip to Center Parcs (could I sound any more fucking middle class?!), I came home to discover him AWOL.

It was with a heavy heart that I announced him missing. My noble steed had been a part of my life for a long and loyal time. Having been sex-toy active since the dawn of my sixteenth birthday, I have come across my fair share of plastic pals, but it is few and far between to get your hands on a really, really good one. Hence my excitement when I met BOB. He was so handsome. Shiny, pink and with interchangeable heads - he was perfect. And, without a doubt, the sole reason for my sexual pleasure and happiness before meeting my current beau. Wherever I have travelled, and whomever I have been with; BOB has always stuck by me. He even graduated to having his own 'travel bag' (a stray sock).

The bond between a woman and her sex toy is without a doubt an unbreakable one. So you can imagine my heartache after the realisation that I had left poor BOB at Center Parcs. Having called multiple times and being repeatedly informed that no one had seen or discovered a perfect, pocket-sized pink pal, I gave up hope. If I told you that I held it together upon uncovering my loss and didn't cry at all, I would be lying. BOB means an awful lot to me. Not only sexually, but sentimentally, and there will be a special place in my heart (and clitoris) reserved for him as long as I shall live and continue to masturbate with him and his ever growing family. Yep, he came back to me. Turns out those hours spent wailing down the phone to the CP customer services team were a waste of time, and I re-located him some weeks later, tucked into a secret pocket of my laptop bag. I can imagine the same sort of bliss and relief being felt upon delivering one's own offspring.

Regardless of relationship status, it is the presence or absence of a vibrating friend that completes the woman. Believe me, I know. And it's no easy feat to partner up with that specific toy that meets all your wants and needs. In fact, it can take years of trial and tribulation.

It's OK to be in a committed relationship and respect your toy. They are allowed to work simultaneously. My boyfriend has a full understanding that my relationship with BOB is nothing short of special, and that we have a frequent desire to spend quality time together. Alternatively, sharing your buzz with your beau is totally OK – I admire a woman who can introduce her two loves to one another and respectfully live her life sans complications. A 2004 Berman Center study titled "Health Benefits of Sexual Aids and Devices" found that 30 percent of couples use vibrators. Sadly, I am not that woman. I have a slightly hysterical problem with sharing BOB (the addictive personality rearing its glorious head again). He is mine only and I value our alone time so highly, that the thought of anyone else interjecting is positively ghastly.

Being so incredibly protective of BOB but yearning for continuous sexual exploration with my partner, we have since invested in multiple toys for mutual use. And it's a game changer. Again, it's cool if you're not open to blurring the boundaries between man and machine. But even if there's an ounce of curiosity about what it might be like, or how it could impact your sexual compatibility, I recommend trying it.

And for my single gals, you can thank me later. Unless you're celibate and don't know what you're missing, you may think you can live without the big O. But give it three to six weeks and you'll be tearing your hair out and/or spending your evenings bathroom bound, distorting your body so the shower head hits it just right. Your magic wand will make everything easier. A Womanizer is perfect for passing the time during Channel 4 ad breaks. Rampant Rabbits brighten even the darkest of Sundays. Regardless of their brand, shape or size, your pleasure product will always be there for you. They won't mind if you've not washed your hair for six days and you're using them without even taking your pyjama bottoms off. They will never talk shit about you to their friends. They wouldn't dream of having too much to drink and being rendered useless. They will ALWAYS be able to perform. And, as a human being, you need that kind of stability in your life. Lest we forget, they can be used at any time, in any (private or semi-so) place and on any part of the body.

Statistically, sex toys boost sexual confidence. They catalyse orgasms, therefore leaving you less stressed and with less of a risk of contracting illness. Trust me, your climax is oh, so good for the body and soul. Purchasing your vibrator is serious business and somewhat of a lifetime investment. Whilst each and every vagina is totally different, reading up on your sex toys reviews is always helpful in making an informed decision. Think about what you want from your vibrator, and peruse. And having the option shop in-store as well as online is a Godsend. Boots have recently launched a 'sexual health and wellbeing' section both online and in-store. Another glorious contribution to what I hope to be a fully sex positive future.

Either way, there are experts to hand to guide you in the right direction. Yes, the sales assistants in Ann Summers serve more purpose than pointing you in the right direction for penis pasta. Said decision is not one to be rushed, so ensure you are completely and totally sure before you purchase your new friend. And, huns, look after your BOBs; you never know when you will experience their last buzz.

I am now the proud mother of a brimming box of BOB's brothers and sisters. And distant cousins in the form of ball gags, studded handcuffs and paddles. The best thing about sex toys is that there is something for everyone; an answer for all kinks (providing they are legal, obviously). There are butt plugs of all colours, shapes and sizes if you're into butt stuff. There are also diamante versions for when you're feeling a little fancy, or if it's a special occasion. Like a wedding. Or a christening. Vibrating undies if you like a public thrill. If you're into being tied up like a rotisserie chicken, there are ropes of almost every variation readily available, and if you like enormous inflatable genitalia, then I have a friend with a costume that would be right up your street – hit me up.

It's also important not to forget that getting to know yourself and your sexuality doesn't have to come from splashing out on toys and gadgets. Anyone has the power to do this in their own home, using their own self. Going back to basics and using your hands and fingers is often a miracle when it comes to improving self-esteem and re-connecting with yourself sexually.

Chapter 32

We should not feel entitled to more than anyone else, simply because our parents shagged within imagined borders, created by beasts of the past and maintained by those of the present.

Here's something a little weird for you all to ponder – meeting new people and experiencing other cultures and religions helped me figure out sex positivity on a massive scale. The most recent of my obsessions is the one I have developed over recent years, circulating exactly that; the celebration of individuality through different cultures, religions and beliefs.

As part of this, and my pending passion for human rights activism, I opted to volunteer with the refugees in Calais. I go with a local group, hailed as the Oxfordshire Refugee Solidarity. I was introduced via some of my girlfriends who had been before, and who were more than happy to give me the required information and details of previous trips they attended. It was a no-brainer for me, and I immediately signed up. Since then, I have been visiting Calais and the surrounding areas whenever possible as part of this most inspirational group.

Whilst I have the opportunity, I would like to dedicate this chapter to my gorgeous friend David Bailey. I made a promise not to mention names throughout this book, but for him I can make an exception. As I write this today, it is a little over a year since David's passing. David introduced me to the wonders of ORS and, without sounding too pretentious, changed my life forever. This man taught me the importance of fighting for what is right, and never giving up. I am eternally grateful for the time I spent with David and for the wisdom and solidarity he imparted. I truly believe that the importance of friendship lies not with how long you've known someone, but the calibre of that person and the quality of your relationship.

To meet someone like David is rare. As human beings, we have a tendency to be egocentric; but not David. Everything he did was for the benefit of another. Whether it be his work as a nurse for the NHS, campaigning for the NHS and Labour or founding and organising the Oxfordshire Refugee Solidarity and our voluntary aid trips to support the refugees in Calais, David is the most selfless person I have ever had the pleasure of meeting. He is calm and kind, and a terrific father to three lovely children, whom he raised solo. Just before Christmas in 2017, David was diagnosed with terminal cancer – proof that terrible things really do happen to the most wonderful, undeserving people. The day he was diagnosed, he boarded a coach to London for a demonstration; epitomising his passion for others.

As a member of the Oxfordshire Refugee Solidarity, I have been privileged enough to fully witness David's amazing acts of kindness on multiple occasions. David makes me want to be a better human. He makes me want to stand up for what I believe in, and for other people. He encourages me to be kind and loving at all times, and to treat other people equally and with respect.

It's time the world knew of David, who he was and what he did. He deserves recognition for his inspirational and noble endeavours and his genuine hard work and dedication to so many causes. He is, to all that know him, the most amazing human.

I was not prepared for my first trip to Calais. Physically, because I hadn't packed thermal layers, a hat or the lifetime's worth of snacks that I ended up consuming, and it was fast approaching December - but mostly, emotionally. I had been spun tales of the people who lived in the woods and the children who were stranded there without family. I had been warned that it was hard to take in but I told myself, imagining it to be on a similar emotional level to watching Comic Relief, that I could handle it. Admittedly, I was nervous during the trip down and on the first morning. Nothing could have prepared me for the initial shock and the utter devastation that human beings are forced to live in such a way. In hindsight, I really should have opted for waterproof mascara.

We are often told that these people 'live in the woods' and images and videos of The Jungle, and a community of tents and huts where these people used to reside, accompany most News coverage. But that was demolished in October 2016, just over a year before my first trip. The people that I have met rarely slept in tents. Their belongings and shelter were ripped away from them daily, following pepper spray attacks by the increasingly violent French authorities. They slept on the ground, under natural accommodation where possible, in all temperatures and weather conditions. They were both desperate for shelter and to move as far away from danger as possible. This basically means that they travel further into abandoned forestry and undergrowth, indeed making it harder to be caught, but also harder to be found by charities on distribution. I have been fortunate enough to spend some time talking with these people and learning of their cultures, stories and backgrounds. The distributions that these people rely on are often for the most basic of amenities, and stuff that you and I wouldn't think twice about. For and to these people, I've helped dish out food, toiletries, socks and shoes, blankets and children's toys, amongst many other things.

I collected sanitary products to take with me on my first trip over. I ended up gathering an entire Corsa full of tampons and pads alike, and was even gifted donations by a truly amazing and ecological sanitary brand, Freda. It was amazing, and I bloody love a project, so my excitement was imaginable. In between bouts of asking my relatives for their unwanted (but clean) sanitary towels and repeatedly begging on Facebook selling sites (turns out the middle aged Tories of Oxfordshire are not my target audience), I would catch my breath and have a minute to think. Can you conceive the idea not having access to the most basic human sanitation? We had hordes of refugees requesting things like deodorant, bottled water and waterproof jackets; again, things that the Western World take so for granted.

Today, take ten minutes. Do it whilst you're on the loo or waiting for the tube or counting down the minutes left until your Chicken Korma is fully microwaved and edible. Think about what it must be like as a young woman, to not only be separated from your family and loved ones, stranded in a cruel and cold place without even the hint of an idea as to what the future holds as far as the next seven days, but also to get your period. We bitch and moan about getting them in the first world. Crying over severe cramps and demanding anything fried or covered in chocolate. Try and think about getting your period and not having access to a shower or a tampon/pad. To be bleeding into the clothes that you will be forced to wear for an uncertain amount of time.

The refugees live in truly brutal conditions that would test even the most resilient of us. They are exhausted, hungry, thirsty, freezing cold, traumatized and desperate. Despite news stories and authority-lead lies, they are not aggressive. If you put any race, creed, gender or nationality under those tense and horrifying conditions for such long periods of time, it's going to test, and even break, the mental health of those involved.

No one deserves luxury before others deserve their life. We should not feel entitled to more than anyone else, simply because our parents shagged within imagined borders, created by beasts of the past and maintained by those of the present. It is sheer dumb luck that we have ended up on the privileged end of society whilst others are denied the most basic human rights. I can no longer pretend that we are civilized species when people are allowed to suffer in this way. When children sleep outside in the freezing cold and snow, and young men turn down an offering of clean, dry walking boots, in case they hinder their trying to run from the police. When, to try and maintain some dignity, people stand at the side of the road and wash and shave in ice cold water and freezing temperatures. When you lie down tonight, in your warm bed and safe home, think of all of those who can't even imagine such luxury and who have to fight every day for hope and life sustaining aid.

I fall in love with almost every human being I meet the other side of the border. I have friends for life in the refugees that we have met. They are kind, patient, polite and charming. They smile and tell jokes. They are lawyers, farmers, engineers, teachers and almost every other profession you could think of. Most have lost beloved family and friends. Some tell heart straining tales of war, famine and enforced national military service. They are human beings, just like us. They try their best to smile and joke - although you can see profound sadness in their eyes. They queue patiently for volunteers to hand out their only source of sustenance. An undignified process for the young, smart and capable individuals who are forced to rely on scarce aid because of the intolerably dangerous situation the world's governments have put them in. They all want to return home to be with their families, in the counties they love. They are in a strange and hostile place. They miss their family, friends, countries and cultures. They want safety but mostly want to be at peace, at home.

These migrants are individuals. They have likes, dislikes, amazing senses of humour, ideas, talents and fabulous quirks. They are us. They are our friends. They are not a threat. Every time I visit Calais, I leave feeling like I have known them forever, and to leave them behind is just heart breaking. The UK's persistent bombing of their countries and selling arms to nourish their wars leaves these people hopeless; stuck in a destitute situation because even that is better than being at home. It takes a certain type of government to persistently bomb a country, and then refuse to taken in their civilians escaping certain death.

The friends that I met in France have given me hope, passion and stories that I will remember forever. Some have made it to the UK, and are now seeking asylum here. Others haven't been so lucky, and are still stuck in French wasteland. One had lived in the UK for eight years. He had a career and a home, and had gone back to his native Afghanistan to visit his dying father, and assist his mother with the funeral plans. Not even three weeks later, he attempted to come back to his home in the UK, and was refused entry. A 17 year old boy told fellow volunteers about the long journey he made through Iran, resulting in him watching two of his sixteen year old friends shot dead in front of him. He also recalled watching the boat ahead of his sinking, and hearing the passengers, mostly women and children, scream and cry out for help as they drowned in the Mediterranean Sea.

There are no words to explain what it's like to leave these people behind when returning from our trip. It is emotional and frightening and you are bidding farewell to gorgeous people that you don't know if you'll ever see again. Every time I've been, I sit and cry through every mile of the homeward journey and for some considerable days afterwards. I always think that it will get better having been on more and more trips, but the disbelief and immense feelings of pain and anger haunt me every time.

We should be celebrating people's cultures – not shaming them for it. Britain is an incredible melting pot of all races and cultures, and it's about time we embraced it. A nation populated by the white middle class doesn't bear thinking about. And I can't imagine there being enough brie and sourdough bread to suffice. We gorge on Indian, Chinese and Italian foods, drink French wine and drive cars predominantly made in Japan and Germany. We interact with various cultures so habitually in our daily lives, so how can we be so against their people?

Racism is a system based on oppression. It's racist to deny these people their rights. Reverse racism is not a thing. You can't be racist to a white person, much like it being impossible to be sexist towards men. Don't get me wrong; you can be prejudiced, rude and discriminatory towards them, but considering the rule of oppression; you cannot be racist or sexist. Men aren't oppressed, and neither are white people.

The group I visit Northern France with have changed my life forever. The sheer kindness and beauty of those who volunteer with and manage the Oxfordshire Refugee Solidarity is dumbfounding. They are amazing and inspirational, and actually, fucking hilarious. It is only with their assistance and support that I continue to have the ability to keep volunteering. And to remember to pack at least a bottle of wine per night that I'm away for. Nothing cures heart ache like getting nice and drunk with likeminded people, and slurring about how much you appreciate your comrades.

Through the people that I've met, and I mean in all of my life so far, I have learnt about how relationships differ among individuals. It goes without saying that, much like genitalia, there is no point in comparing your relationship to anyone else's as they are, and are meant to be, completely fucking different. Particularly through meeting people with different backgrounds and beliefs.

Chapter 33

The practises and beliefs of sex vary so considerably between cultures.

Sex is arguably an important part in most relationships. Physical intercourse is one of those things, interpreted completely differently among individuals and different cultures. For me, sex couldn't be more important. Aside from the fact that writing about it is my passion, my sex drive is at an abnormal high. So it's more than likely that I am the exception to the particular rule in just how much sex one should be having whilst in a relationship. Not that there even is a 'rule'. I strongly believe that each individual person is different and their bodies are just that – different. All relationships are completely unique, and this is just one of the many, many reasons why you'll never benefit from relating yours to anyone else's. Whilst some (mentioning no names...) find themselves persistently nagging their boyfriends for some action hourly, some only fancy a dicking once a month.

My loving chap and I probably get down and dirty

once a week – twice if I'm really lucky. Normally this revolves around a hungover Sunday, where we drift in and out of naps and binge watch Netflix while paying each other's nether regions some serious attention and inhaling toast. And, whilst this is more than the national average, I often can't help but want more. It's probably not completely accurate to compare our current sex life with that we had at the beginning of our relationship. The 'honeymoon period' typically lasts for the first three to six months of a relationship. This aptly named phase stems from those sacred, initial feelings of lust, passion and even love. So, essentially, when you've fancied someone for ages and finally get to have your wicked way with them on the reg feels pretty amazing. It's more than just shagging, though. It's spending your time with someone new, learning about their lives, ordering pizza every second night and piling on some considerable kgs. As a couple, we followed suit. 'Sore dick Sundays' became a regular occurrence, with our record number of shags skyrocketing to twelve in twelve hours. Ah, the good old days.

In truth, I think our relationship is significantly stronger when our sex life is frequent. I'm not referring to the verging on unnatural dozen-a-day shagathons, but to at least twice a week. For me, it's important to feel involved with someone and that happens a lot through physical intimacy. The Spice Girls were definitely on to something with '2 Become 1'. That is how sex in a relationship should make you feel; connected. My boyfriend doesn't believe me when I tell him vaginal sex, for me, is the most intimate. Of course, he argues his point after trying to slip it into my arsehole for the third time that morning.

To me, the stereotypical, slightly misogynistic view that men constantly think with their dick and are almost always looking to get it wet is slightly askew. I'm horny a lot more frequently than my boyfriend is, and I know many of my gal pals feel the same. Sure, in some relationships sex drive is male dominated, but it would be impossible (backwards and basically, fucking stupid) to categorize libido by gender.

I cannot be the only one who remembers that documentary about the 80-something couple who were still having sex? How the effing eff did that make for lucrative viewing? The idea of getting to a certain age and then just never having sex again fills me with a body-numbing fear. Given that I am, at present, the Queen of nag town after two days without the D. And how would you know which was to be your last hoorah? Is it something ordinarily planned in advance? Is it standard to arrange a special fireworks ceremony for the eventual climax and a spelling of 'RIP sex life' across the sky? Or does it happen naturally? Personally, I'm more inclined to opt for option number 1, so I can make sure to have plucked out any stray bikini hairs and donned the Granny equivalent to matching, saucy lingerie. My best silk, full-bottomed pants and ankle-skimming 100% cotton M&S nightie, perhaps. Either way, I want my last time to be memorable for all involved.

Alongside my cock-loving friends, I also associate with those saving themselves for the big day. For many religions and cultures, it is seen as impure to give away your flower to anyone other than your husband on the night of your wedding. So many people turn their nose up at the idea – but can you really even miss something you never had? Granted, this might not be the best example, but those who have been a vegetarian since birth don't often miss the taste of meat. In truth, I admire the dedication of 'withholding'. Self-control is a gift – take it from someone who spends their Friday nights crawling home at 4am after going for that one quick after work drink with the girls.

But that speaks volumes alone. So many cultures bearing the view that sex is SO sacred in a relationship that it should be worked for and cherished surely supports the argument that it is the ultimate goal – to intermingle not only mind, but also body. For two people in love, having sex adds a new and incredible depth to their coupling. Perhaps that's why it's most often referred to as 'making love'. People have very different opinions on what abstinence is, but it is usually reference to refraining from any and all sexual acts. Whilst sex may be off the table, most couples still engage in cuddling, kissing, or holding hands. In complete contradiction to the religious belief process on sex acts such as masturbation, abstinence is said to relate to purity because it highlights one's commitment to their specific God. Some Catholic sects believe that the sole reason for sex is procreation and should not be taken advantage of for pleasure, so opt to take virginity pledges until legally married. Obviously, the belief that abstinence is effective is not culture-wide. The Dutch actually have a very liberal society that does not emphasize abstinence in any of its forms. They do, however, highlight the importance of teaching communication among partners so that sex is comfortable for all involved. Yet another reason to look into moving to Amsterdam.

Getting busy statistically contributes to a happier individual through the release of endorphins, making your relationship inevitably stronger, and funding a more connected partnership. Perhaps more so than anything else, sharing something so natural and raw with your other half makes you feel cherished and happy. Note that these particular results apply solely to couples who sustain a physical bond and not with those choosing to abstain. Nonetheless, with an insatiable emotional bond, there is no real reason you couldn't continue a happy, loving relationship with the absence of a sex life. Some may be able to get on board with the idea, while some (namely me) would sit back, horrified at the thought. Essentially, every couple has an entirely individual relationship – hence why I disagree with comparing yours to anyone else's.

Reiterating, one couple might be more than happy to butter the biscuit but once a year, whilst another would prefer a daily performance. Regardless, it is your decision to make concerning what works for you. Sex may not be the be-all and end-all, after all.

I'm sure this goes without saying, but any verdict regarding your relationship should be made with a meeting of the minds. It's not a decision to be taken lightly or made alone – your other half might just have something to say if you swear yourself off intercourse for eleven months of the year without so much of an explanation. Honesty is always the best policy and in any relationship, communication is key. Saying this, sex shouldn't be something you have to pre-plan. I'm yet to see a happy couple who maintain a scheduled sex life. Can you imagine tallying up intercourse on a spreadsheet taped to the back of your kitchen door? "Well done, darling – 45 seconds longer than last week! Gold star for you!"

Learning about the ways other people view sex has been a turning point in my life and the way that I look at intercourse. Regardless of where you are from or who your God is, most of us think of us understand the concept of sex as a ceremonious act. And it absolutely is. We might not use the same words to describe it, but it really does all boil down to the power of being physically intimate with a loved one, and potentially creating new life. I think there's actually something pretty beautiful about making the physical act of intimacy such a big deal, and I'm probably going to go home now and set up a shrine dedicated to my sex life.

Whilst I am in sheer admiration of some, there are also those beliefs that I just can't wrap my head around. Providing it is consensual, I am of no opposition, but the idea of an arranged marriage baffles me. Probably due to the same reasons that I can't get my head around chastity and saving yourself for marriage, but that's just me. Marriage is something which takes many forms across different cultures and is on a vast spectrum shaped by traditions and values. An arranged marriage is when partners are chosen for each other by other family members or guardians, usually without any input from the soon-to-be-married individuals. Imagine having you mum or dad pick your partner for you! It doesn't bear thinking about. These situations usually occur where families agree to terms for items, monetary value, or power.

Arranged marriages are typically not very common in Western cultures whereas, in countries like Afghanistan, it is common for a female under 16 years of age to be strategically married off. This doesn't sit quite so well with me. If it's part of your religion and you have knowingly and happily entered into an arranged marriage then fine. But if you're forced into anything, sold or traded or married off underage, I am so not on board. Correct me if I'm wrong, but shouldn't we be able to make our own decisions in the twenty first century?

The practises and beliefs of sex vary so considerably

between cultures. You might think of kissing as one of the most basic sources of sexual arousal in Western society, unless of course you're losing your virginity to a man from South Oxon. Believe it or not, the locking of lips is often uncommon or completely absent in many other cultures. It's a little alien to me, admittedly, as I am almost always pissing my boyfriend off by persistently kissing him all over his face and demanding snogs morning, noon and night.

In our Western ways, the exchange of a kiss is most commonly used as a sign of greeting, love, friendship, passion, or romance. Whilst mouth-to-mouth kissing is seen as very common in Western and European cultures, in cultures like the Thonga Tribe of South Africa, it is viewed negatively. In a recent study, researchers tested the presence of romantic kissing across 168 cultures and found that only 77 of these cultures (46%) practiced romantic kissing. Some people may think that kissing is commonplace, but it is statistically more common to avoid romantic kissing in a culture than it is to engage in. For example, in some states in India, people have gathered to protest by kissing in public as a way of going against the cultural stigma that surrounds the act.

Some cultures have other means of affection that can be compared to kissing, such as an "Eskimo kiss," which requires partners to rub their noses together. This reminds me of the greeting my Goddaughter and I used to practice, although a lot more snotty. Adorable, right? Among the cultures that kiss, many people (mostly

Europeans and posh boys from Oxfordshire) simply choose to kiss on one or both cheeks as a greeting to friends and family. The Greeks greet each other with non-romantic mouth-to-mouth kissing. I'm here for it. My last name actually translates to 'relating to Greek', and everything makes so much sense now.

WOMAN UP

Chapter 34

Sex positivity, much like feminism in general, is all inclusive and never prejudiced.

I pray to each and every God that if you're sexually active, you know what foreplay is. It's the necessary sexual interaction between partners in the lead up to sex. Recently, I found out that it takes between 20 – 40 minutes of pre-performance pursuit before a woman can get a vaginal stiffy and be open to full orgasmic potential. Typically, this consists of kissing and stimulation or arousal of the sexual organs and erogenous zones. Or, if you're fornicating with some of the men from my home town, it means breathing heavily down your neck whilst they spend a fortnight trying to locate your clitoris. #Vadryna.

Foreplay is the trailer in the lead up to the main movie. You can do one without the other, but it's not preferable. Many Eastern societies engage in foreplay for extended periods of time, as they too strive to prolong sexual arousal. At the same time, many cultures (including ones found within Western and Eastern societies) engage in limited amounts of foreplay, or foreplay is completely absent. Where I come from, foreplay is essential; whether you're accepting of the fact or not. Sex isn't necessarily all about dicks and vag and penetration. Please, stop being so lazy and utilise the other gifts that the good lord gave you. Kissing me once on the mouth and then entering dry is just not my kink.

My boyfriend sometimes seems to think he can get me in the mood by rubbing his erection on my leg and spooning me with one hand on my breast. Forgive me, darling, if I'm getting just a little tired of you rolling over out of nowhere and thrusting into me with no prior warning. In Western cultures, varied patterns of foreplay can be found, but these all tend to be short in duration and to be seen as something that leads up to the "main event" of intercourse. Furthermore, some cultures have a completely different definition of foreplay than most cultures. For example, partners from the Trobrian Islanders of Melanesia typically exchange saliva and bite each other's lips until they bleed as a way of increasing sexual arousal.

One of my very favourite foreplay practises is oral sex. Oral sex can be a very erotic preview that leads to sex, or it can be its own "main event", bringing sexual pleasure, satisfaction, and hopefully even orgasms to its beneficiaries. Turns out, it's not just something you're asked to do by arrogant men who think that physically guiding your head towards their crotch will automatically make you interested in sucking them off.

Especially in our society, oral sex has become common. It is the norm to perform and, reportedly, one of our Nation's favourite porn categories. In various other cultures, putting your mouth near anyone's genitals is deemed taboo or morally wrong. Namely, some African cultures view cunnilingus and felatio to be highly unnatural, and many religions across the world look upon this act as a sin.

I'm also kind of really, really into masturbation, if you hadn't already grasped. Ever since discovering it when I was probably too young, I have been obsessed with my downstairs and, whilst somewhat overdramatic, I wouldn't be true to myself if I claimed I could live without it. I can barely go a few days without it, for crying out loud. Seriously, don't chat to me if I've been without BOB for longer than 72 hours. A week's holiday was once ruined by his absence. So it deeply saddens me that so many cultures disapprove of masturbation. Many condemn on religious grounds, considering it sinful and professing that desire should be reduced at all costs. While others suggest that masturbation is relatively harmless and may even be beneficial.

There is no mistaking that pleasuring yourself is a completely natural phenomenon. It's laughable that, in attempt to rid their following of any want for sexual pleasure, certain religions promote the negative side effects of masturbation to be digestive pains, spine damage, reproductive damage, mental disorders, and insanity. It's total bullshit, and none of which have ever been scientifically proved. Quite the opposite, in fact. Doing the five finger shuffle or engaging in a little ménage à moi can have huge benefits to your health. Including but not limited to: boosting self-esteem, promoting better sleep patterns, strengthening pelvic and anal muscles and even relieving menstrual tension and cramping. You just can't argue with the facts.

Same-sex love has always been a controversial topic, specifically in more recent years and with older generations. Owing to support from LGBTQ+ rights groups and campaigns across the world, acceptance is at an all time high. We're still not there yet, but we are on our way and you'd better believe that I'm all for bringing my children up in a world promoting love – regardless of who or what said love is between. If you're still in any doubt of whether or not you're in approval of same sex lovers, treat yourself to an evening watching *Queer Eye*. It will change your life. I sincerely hope they get to read this and make me the straight, chubby best friend that they never knew they needed. Plus that would put a stop to my constant direct Instagram messages, begging them to accept me as one of their own and teach me how to make a fancy grilled cheese.

Fun fact - in ancient Japan and at the time of the Samurai, it was not uncommon for men to have partners of the same sex, who were required to be loyal until their deaths. Back in September 2013, the Pope made a statement claiming that God does not condemn homosexuals. Seeing as a billion of the earth's population is Catholic, his message had significant impact. When the Pope changed his position from that of condemnation to acceptance, a cultural movement was spurred, likely influencing the legalization of gay marriage in America in 2015.

Slightly ahead of the game that was already far too late, the UK legalised the conversion of civil partnerships to legal marriages the year prior. A triumph, indeed; but still something to think about. How on earth did it take so long for this to come into play? We know that various sexualities have been around since the dawn of time, and Pride festivals made their debut in 1970. As shocking as it is that people have only been able to wed who they wish for a few years, there are still various communities worldwide who denounce this, and even here in the UK there have been recent protests over gay relationships being shown in school textbooks.

Most of us would consider marriage to be a legally binding communion between two partners, but there are so many people and places, such as some districts in India, that still practice polygamy and polyandry. A percentage of Muslim residents in Malaysia and the Philippines also allow and support polygamy, while having more than one partner in Western culture is certainly not the done thing. Not publicly, anyway. Another aspect of marriage that intersects with cultural norms is tolerance for monogamy. You know how I feel about the M word. Monogamy is defined as having an agreement with one's partner about an exclusive relationship. In Thailand, it is commonplace to willingly commit adultery, whilst in Ireland, the Catholic community would deem cheating as immoral. Gender and sex currently play a key role in legal marriage. Some cultures approve of homosexuality while others condemn it. I, for one, can't wait to move to Non-Binary Island where we will all be free to snog, marry and avoid whomever we wish.

I can't ramble on about different cultures and the way they view sex and relationships without touching on physical rendering of body parts. Removal of the foreskin of the penis, typically referred to as circumcision, is ritualistic as it is discussed in biblical texts. There is some scientific evidence that supports male circumcisions; the Center for Disease Control and Prevention (CDC) in the United States cites studies that claim men who are circumcised are much more protected against HIV infections as well as other sexually transmitted infections. But inevitably it boils down to religion. My personal preference, having seen just about every kind of penis under the sun? Whatever they want. Circumcision should probably be a decision best left until the possessor is of a reasonable age to make their own decision. A bit like piercing a baby's ears. Is it worth putting your baby through pain just to improve their aesthetics?

FGM, or female genital mutilation, is the alteration or removal of female genitalia. Mostly performed on little girls. Nearly 200 million females have been victims of FGM across the world. Not all cultures perform genital-altering procedures but the cultures that do tend to believe that it is traditional, cleaner, a necessary rite of passage to womanhood, a prevention for promiscuity and the promise of better marriage prospects as a result of enhanced male sexual pleasure. The majority of these procedures are carried out in more than half of the African countries, Asia and the Middle East. Unsurprisingly, this is predominantly a forced procedure, intensely painful and, inevitably, leads to more harm than good through infection, blood loss or complications. Whilst these issues might not cross your mind on a day to day basis, it's time we stopped ignoring matters that don't appear to be happening on our doorstep. Because they are.

FGM is a worldwide phenomenon. It is everywhere. It has been outlawed in the UK since 1985, but statistically over 114,000 girls in England and Wales are at current risk. Between April 2015 and March 2016, there were 5,702 new cases in England. And these are only those reported. The numbers are huge, and yet Britain's second trial fell through in March 2019. The first to be tried for this barbaric crime? A respected doctor from a London hospital. It would be naïve to believe that FGM is not practiced in your home countries.

The hymen is a thin piece of skin that covers the vaginal opening and protects the vagina. It's meant to be the tell-tale sign of a virgin, even though you can break it doing a multitude of activities that aren't sexual penetration; horse riding and tampon insertion, for example. The cultural significance of the hymen is much more complicated than its role in the body. Many traditional cultures and religions see the hymen as a symbol of purity and virginity. A lot of cultural stigmas resides around the hymen because virginity is prized in patriarchal societies that require women to be sexually restrictive, while men can do whatever they please. A surgical process called a hymenoplasty is used to repair females' hymens so that they seem like virgins again, but this process is mainly used in cultures where virginity is highly prized, such as in China. Although there are ideological extremes regarding the hymen, there are other cultures that do not regard the hymen as important at all.

We can only truly accept and integrate sex positivity once we have done so for every culture, religion and weirdo on the tube. Sex positivity, much like feminism in general, is all inclusive and never prejudiced. If you're at all confused or there is something blocking your path to sex positive-ness, then make it known. Ask questions, process the answers and, for crying out loud, get on board.

Chapter 35

Sex work is real work, and should be treated and respected as such.

Similarly to fighting for the reproductive and equal rights of women, it's high time we decriminalise sex work. Want to stop human trafficking? Decriminalise the sex industry. Under legalisation, sex work would be controlled by the government and legality determined by state and country-specific conditions. Decriminalising would remove all prostitution specific laws, but still allow sex workers and businesses to operate, providing they do so within the laws of the land. I've been to Amsterdam, and I love it. It's a glorious city, and one of the most notorious for hosting legal brothels. And coffee shops, but that's a story for another day.

The Red Light District tends to perplex me. Part of me wants to run screaming into the brothels, and free all the workers as if they were some sort of caged animal awaiting slaughter. And then there's a huge part of me that feels completely empowered. These women are taking business and sexuality into their own hands.

The only issue surrounding sex work are pimps and unfavourable clientele. I think, and bear with me here, that if a prostitute strictly does all they can to keep themselves safe; security and regular health checks etc, then they should be allowed to practice as they see fit.

New Zealand are the only country to have fully decriminalised sex work so far. As reported by researchers, vendors both working on the street and from indoors claim to have stronger relationships with the authorities, and as a result feel safer. Those conducting business indoors are within legal rights to take their employers to court. So let's treat prostitution as what it really is; a business. It's a profession like almost any other and, in the internet age, is hard to hide from anyone (despite how hard the powers that be have tried). What consenting adults do behind closed doors, whether paying for it or not, should be of no concern to anyone else. If y'all want safety for 'people of the night' and, as mentioned, a decrease in human trade, this would considerably assist in the breaking up of pimps and trafficking gangs. Human trafficking and sex slaves are more common than you'd ever know. They are prosperous and growing, largely as a result of these activities being illegal. Everything is done 'underground' and through the black market. If regulated, the government can emplace regulations on business, making it harder for these things to occur.

When alcohol was illegal, people found access to it through mobs and gangs. When porn was illegal, they did the same. Since the dawn of laws against non-prescription drugs, users have still had access to getting what they wish. And just how do you think that happens? Gold star, you win; through gang based criminals. It's exactly the same for sex work. As it stands in our country, there is no safe and easy way to pay for sex. The moment we change prostitution law is the moment that these people will no longer be able to collect profit off them. Sex work is real work, and should be treated and respected as such.

Prostitution has existed since the dawn of humanity. It is the world's longest standing trade. Did you know that globally, the prostitution business is worth around $186 billion? If this were abiding by tax laws, imagine how much our economy could benefit. Transforming this industry into an organised trade would be beneficial to almost all involved, including the diminishment of the constant threat of violence.

Let's not preach about rape culture and sex positivity and then contradict ourselves by trying to control activity between two consenting adults. This is an industry that, regardless of whether it's legal or not, is still practiced and always will, because human beings have natural needs. If a man has that need and wants to visit a prostitute; he is not harming anyone, he is an adult with personal responsibility and should not be denied to spend his money as he so wishes. You wouldn't kick off about someone splashing out on Dom Pérignon if they had the money to do it? You definitely wouldn't be complaining if they offered you a glass. In principle, it's the same. Fulfilling a need or desire. As for the workers themselves, this is a job. Some use their natural skills to make a living, some use their intellectuality and some use their bodies. Providing everyone abides by the rules and looks after themselves, it's fairly harmless. If you want sex, there should be no shame in visiting a prostitute and exchanging money for a service. This is the exact definition of market and what makes our economic system thrive.

Last but absolutely not least, the most popular reason that prostitution is illegal and carrying such a negative reputation, is its status for being immoral. Somewhat bizarrely, people don't want their children growing up in a world with less sexual violence and crime and more consensual and widely discussed sexual activity. For anyone in disagreement, the only real way you'll ever keep people away from things you find immoral is by ridding the stigma and crime that surrounds it, don't you agree?

Chapter 36

***I literally refuse to be given orders,
unless it's mid-consensual shag.***

I am a feminist, we know this. I'm also somewhat of a nymphomaniac, we now all know this too. I am working on sex positivity and getting people to talk about it like it's the perfectly natural human behaviour and necessary means of population that it is. And I appreciate that sex for everyone is a completely different experience, and all those who either are or aren't sexually active have their own thoughts, opinions, kinks and desires. I like a bit of rough and tumble in the bedroom, and am not opposed to some light BDSM. But, apparently, as a feminist, it is wrong to be partial to a little bedroom choking. BDSM is not about abuse. It is fully consensual (hence the use of safe words). Films like *50 Shades* depict this in completely the wrong light; actively encouraging its readers and viewers that stalking, isolating, pressurising and raping your partner are all safely under the bondage umbrella. They are not.

Judging anyone on their consensual sex lives is

patriarchal. I'm a fan of being submissive. Perhaps a result of being so domineering in every aspect of my life other than the bedroom, but when being intimate, I like to be spanked, held down and have my hair pulled - amongst various other things. I am perfectly demonstrating the mutual co-existence of feminism and dom/sub sex.

This is probably a good place to point out that 'regular' sex isn't a thing. You can have perfectly pleasurable vanilla, mostly-missionary sex, but the term regular adheres to the ideal that having a specific kink (or kinks) isn't normal. When, actually, in fact, it's something embraced by almost every sexual being. We just need to learn how to talk about it. It needs to be more than public knowledge that legal and consensual sex of any kind is OK. It's OK to talk about and it's OK to partake in. I struggle to locate scenarios in which the terms 'regular' and 'normal' are ok. In literally all aspects of life, we are individual and different, and should not be conned into behaving in certain ways just because we think that if everyone else is doing it, it must be right.

We need to make new rules. You cannot judge people on their sexual preferences. I am not any less of a feminist because I want to be dominated. And the fact that I'm into rough sex, doesn't excuse my rapist's behaviour, despite what the police may have told me. My sexual precedence was not determined by my assault. I did not develop a sudden fetish for the thin line between pleasure and pain because of one man's taking advantage of me. That's not how this works.

I will chose who I give my body to, and how I do so. The only other being who could ever even warrant being part of the situation, is that human that I am sharing myself with. I am empowered by my fetishes; and so should you. Being told what to do and punished for misbehaving excites me, because there's almost no other situation that I would allow that to happen in. I literally refuse to be given orders, unless it's mid-consensual shag.

From what I've learned from those shitty sex ed classes, having un-protected sex will ultimately lead to a baby. You'll soon read my stance on women not choosing to be a mum, but it is a broader spectrum than that.

We've got to start talking about abortion. Regardless of whether or not you've been in the situation, it's imperative to certify that it's OK. Being pro-choice doesn't mean you don't care for the life of an unborn foetus. It means you care for the living, breathing human that carries it, and her right to make a choice. People across the globe actually think that shutting down clinics is going to abolish abortion forever. As in, getting rid of birth control and the methods that people use to stop themselves getting pregnant, is going to make sure that everyone who ever has an egg fertilised is going to want to be a mother. Yeah, right.

I love babies, and I would find it difficult to terminate considering how desperate I am for a remake of *The*

Sound of Music to be made based on my life, but I support my sisters and I want them to have the option to opt out of motherhood for whatever reason; be it unfortunate timing, economic climate or something more sinister. Being pro-choice isn't just about supporting the legal right to an abortion. It's also fighting to keep legal celibacy and abstinence, contraception use (both emergency and not so) and childbirth.

"I am pro-abortion like I'm pro-knee-replacement and pro-chemotherapy and pro-cataract surgery. As the last protection against ill-conceived childbearing when all else fails, abortion is part of a set of tools that help women and men to form the families of their choosing. I believe that abortion care is a positive social good. I suspect that a lot of other people secretly believe the same thing. And I think it's time we said so." – *Valerie Tarico, Salon.com.*

My girl Val's got a point. In fact, she's got THE point. She understands that women who lack the means to manage their fertility lacks the means to manage her life. And it really is that simple. If I hadn't had access to contraceptives, I would likely be the mother of an entire brood. But, at sixteen when I became sexually active, that wasn't an option for me. I was still at school. I was still calling my mother when home alone to ask how to boil pasta – I actually couldn't even look after myself. Having a baby would never have been a feasible option.

We are lucky to have access to such a wide variety of contraception. There are an abundance of pills, two types of coil, injections, condoms (for both men and women) and an implant. As well as preventing unwanted pregnancies, each contraceptive boasts a load of other benefits too. Condoms help prevent sexually transmitted diseases, and hormone-based routes can contribute to regulating periods and assisting with acne. They reduce the risk of developing certain reproductive cancers and are often prescribed to help various other menstrual related symptoms and disorders.

All benefits aside, I'm not sure why it's fallen as a woman's responsibility to protect herself from pregnancy. How about you do something to keep your sperm controlled? It takes two to make a baby. They have the option of wearing a condom, but that's it. A contraceptive pill designed for men was actually invented, but pulled because of side effects including weight gain. Yes, you read correctly. Men couldn't deal with gaining an extra few lbs, and so it's been left up to us women to take the hit, again. And no one's racing to find an alternative pill to curb our common side effects; weight gain, water retention, nausea, dizziness, breast tenderness, headaches and vomiting.

At this exact moment in time, I'm not taking any contraception. I'm applying the trusty old 'pull out' method (this isn't actually at all trusty, so please don't take my word) and winging it. Not the smartest move I've ever made, but I came to a point where filling my body with the same fake hormones that it had endured for the past eight years became too much. I am looking towards other options, and donning our rubber friends in the meantime.

I have no idea how long I had chlamydia for before I was tested, both times. Please get tested two weeks after every one night stand! It takes approximately twelve days for your fanny to feel funny after you may or may not have contracted something. Getting swabbed before then is a waste of time, because nothing would show up. You'd have given up half an hour to have someone platonically poke around your bits for nothing. So get tested two weeks, and then three months after. Or just set up a rolling reminder to make regular appointments. That way, you cover all bases and stay as safe as possible.

Plus you get free condoms with every trip to the clinic; the grown up's version of a sticker from the dentist. It's free, and leaving such infections untreated can actually cause infertility. I am terrified that I won't be able to have children. It's my worst fear, and I feel like I've had too many unprotected encounters and not enough morning after pills – so surely I should have been pregnant by now? I have, twice. And I've miscarried both times very early on. But I fear that there's something not quite right, and when the time comes, I'll struggle to conceive. Thinking about it sends me into full panic mode. The only thing I've wanted consistently for my entire life is to be a mum; and I know I'd be really amazing at it. Can't you just picture it now? Me with my brood of tiny feminists? Adorable. I won't overthink any further, as I'm fairly sure that's where the panic initiated in the first place, but take it from someone who knows. Use contraception and get tested.

WOMAN UP

Chapter 37

My bastard little ovaries are ganging up on me.

I have polycystic ovary syndrome (PCOS), and it seems I'm not alone.

My bastard little ovaries are ganging up on me. It's somewhat a pain in the arse, given that the advisory lifestyle changes include avoiding wine and potatoes (two of my most staple food groups), but a real relief that I finally have an answer to my questions. Earlier this year, I started noticing some changes. I was putting on weight for no apparent reason, I had severe bloating that nothing would shift, my skin was oily and I was breaking out constantly. I've always been quite a hairy person, but the level of thick dark hairs on my body started to creep up and then, finally, my periods decided they had better things to do than pay me regular visits. After multiple pregnancy panics I was finally referred for a scan. The next day, they confirmed my diagnosis.

I can't say much else about it at this point, because it's a relatively recent discovery. But I have decided to attempt some lifestyle changes in the form of eating less bread (actually wept at the initial thought), drinking less wine, consuming less sugar overall and attempting to pack in my beloved cigarettes. Oh, and I'm drinking some foul tasting probiotic every morning and taking an abundance of supplements. Basically, I just need a little detox so my ovaries decide they like me again.

Sometimes the thought of PCOS terrifies me. Sometimes I feel fine. When I first had an inkling that it could be the diagnosis (after weeks of googling), I struggled massively with the idea. Because, as I'm sure you're all aware when googling any symptoms, I was being dealt the 'worst case scenario' outcomes. Which, in my case, were diabetes, heart disease, certain types of endometrial cancer and infertility. And I can't wait to have babies. Anyone who knows me will tell you, I have been broody since I was about 7 years old and the world without my future feminist offspring sounds pretty shit to me. So, that was my biggest fear. But I am 25. I have been reassured that, providing I look after myself and don't wait until I'm verging on menopausal to procreate, I should be OK.

Part of my current plan is to round up any and all local fellow polysisters (get it?!), partly because I need a friend or two to support me and listen to me whinge about the lack of Pinot Grigio in my bloodstream and partly because it's gotta be easier to face with an army of bad-ass bitches behind you. Seriously, though. Stuff like this is always made easier with a support system and people who are willing to listen to your problems and share theirs. We women need each other, because otherwise I'll be stuck with my boyfriend who keeps rubbing my lower stomach while making pitiful faces towards it and ostensibly forgetting my lifestyle changes and buying me cake.

WOMAN UP

Chapter 38

*I do not like the word 'virgin'.
In relation to both cocktails and sex.*

We are a pretty selfish generation. I'm here for it, other than when we are so focused with ourselves that we miss out on noticing the crucial differences among us as a population. I think opening one's eyes is a life lesson everyone should adopt. It's well established that sex is totally different among different people. From a kiss on both cheeks to the breaking of a hymen; it's user specific.

In very simple, technical terms, the definition of virginity loss is the penetration of a vagina using a penis, and therefore the diminishment of the 'seal' to both your vagina and your sex life. Hip, hip, hooray – and you're open for business. But is it really that simple? I just don't believe penetration is the only factor in which a virginity can be taken. I mean, I don't believe in virginity as a whole, but I'll humour the professionals just this once. It is impossible for us all to lose our virginities if there is only one possible way to lose it. As much as it pains me to be attracted to men, I am - but some people just don't like dick. You couldn't possibly force a male lover on a lesbian, just so she could be considered no longer a virgin? Let's say that you using and losing your V card is just down to the first time you're sexually intimate with a partner, penetration or not.

I would also like to extend this to literally anyone or any sexuality. I invite anyone with a low or absent sexual attraction to other people to take their own virginity. It's scientifically proven that you can, so why the fuck not? If we're out to smash social constructs, why not add virginity to the hit list.

Furthermore, virginity is typically associated with sex. Again, mostly penetrative, but there has never been much speculation around whether or not you can ditch your virginity having oral sex. The argument here would be based loosely around the hymen. But this would then only apply to women losing their virginities and, if we're all striving for equality, with this particular belief system, it becomes so much more of the useless flap of skin that it is. I think virginity, if at all, should refer to the interaction with any and all sexual organs. So, if you want to count that time your next door neighbour oozed your noodle, then so be it.

I do not like the word 'virgin'. In relation to both cocktails and sex. It has such negative and child-like connotations attached to it which, for a damned if you do, damned if you don't situation, is barely worth wasting your time over. I understand the medical use of the word, and resulting application in other walks of life, but we should stop using it to label and discriminate against people.

Other than my brief and intense fling with the carrot, I lost my virginity three months before my 17th birthday. Often, when telling the story, I am met with shock that I was so old at the time of fornicating for the first time. It's almost as if my 'no fucks' personality and penchant for penis have made it seem as though I exited the womb looking for dick. I mean, it's totally true, but I don't like to appear too predictable.

Sex is subjective. Always. Sex is about personal preference and context. As I've said, our culture, media, peers et al continuously push this idea upon us that having real sex means having intercourse (automatically invalidating any and all non cis hetero sexual experiences), and doing literally anything else is foreplay, and something to rush through before you get to the actual sex bit of sex. Which is, of course, complete and utter bollocks.

Intercourse is simply a preference. It is not the definition of sex. Outercourse, if you will, can be just as fulfilling, exciting and sexy. You're totally forgiven if, at this moment, you feel like you've been subconsciously limiting yourself through assumptions about what real sex actually is. Give yourself a break and the permission to explore. Have all kinds of sex and discover your true personal preferences. Take control of your pleasure. What a fucking magical thing to be able to do.

My first fling with his thing was during my second

'date' with a boy five years older and half an inch taller than me. I know his height doesn't actually add anything to this sordid tale, but I want you to have all necessary details for optimum visualisation. We watched South Park (a classic romance, if you're not already familiar) and, before I knew it, one thing was leading to another and my (at the time VERY cool) SpongeBob printed girl boxers were making their descent. Dreamy, huh? Especially given that he never kissed me. Well, nothing other than a peck anyway. And to think that I dated a man who wouldn't kiss me on the lips for a considerable portion of my sixteenth year. Pretty Woman, who?

At 16, I was not the body positive goddess that I am now, believe it or not. Probably four stone lighter than I am to this day, and I honestly believed that I looked as though I had eaten a small village. Like, what? I would persistently whinge about carbs finding me, regardless of how hard I tried to hide, and even asked how many sit ups I would have to do before I looked like a Kardashian. I wasn't carrying any extra weight. Nothing that I shouldn't have been thrilled to carry, anyway. But losing my virginity at the same time as struggling with my body image was somewhat of a cataclysmic internal riot.

I looked pretty damn hot. I still do, mind, those four stone have treated me well. I online shopped for sexy lingerie, and sent it back believing I looked like pork crackling doused in lace (sounds really bloody tasty, actually) when I had a beautiful body. Every once in a while, though, I would pack in weeping over my ever-expanding arm circumference, throw caution to the wind and play deep throat with an extra-large hot dog and cheese fries. And then I started to realise that iceberg lettuce will never make me as happy as a pepperoni pizza would. I was torturing myself and denying my favourite person happiness because I thought that my life would fall into place if I once again fit into the pyjama bottoms I wore when I was 13.

You think the shagging would've distracted me, at the very least. But I have clear and painful memories of panicking about how my naked body looked in the light and carefully opting for the salad-based option on our dates (another loose term - we went to Nandos once).

WOMAN UP

Chapter 39

The only person you ever need to worry about is yourself, and the love that you have for the way you are.

It took me a really long time to find peace with how I look. I have dieted on and off for the last ten years. That's an entire decade of my life spent worrying about what other people would think of me if I didn't look a certain way or, indeed, adhere to society's 'perfect girl' image. I have always been the bigger girl. As a baby, you could've mistaken me for the Michelin man and I grew up with baby fat which never seemed to want to leave me. I mean, I get it – my thick thighs are so glorious, I don't blame them for never wanting to be apart. But I didn't always feel that way – queue mental images emerging of me, aged 16, angling my pictures and standing with my feet metres apart and bum stuck out like it's no-one's business, trying my hardest to elude that I might have a thigh gap.

Diet culture is something so prominent, in the younger generations specifically, and yet something seldom talked about. Dieting isn't body positive. We know that. No one should feel shamed into losing or gaining weight. And, honestly, nothing is more annoying than an Instagram feed boasting pictures of Herbalife breakfast shakes and bread-less brunches. I believe social pressure in the form of diet advice and before and after pictures to be somewhat damaging and ultimately suggestive that it is the norm to want to change and alter your body rather than being happy and comfortable within yourself.

Before 2017, I constantly scrutinized what I ate and whenever I 'treated' myself (for 72 hour binges most weekends), I would live in guilt and juice for days afterwards. And, admittedly, would then post before and after pictures with a 'look how hot and skinny I look' subcontext. All in all? Not a healthy lifestyle. It wasn't until I realised that buying a size 8 rather than a size 14 wouldn't make me any happier (this is purely an example, the last time I was a size 8, I WAS 8) and that the only way for me to lose 10lbs would be to amputate a vital limb, that I decided to ditch the diets.

And you know what I've learned since? It's OK if I'm not your type! News flash, there will never be one person out there who fancies a slice of every pie – you get me? Some people like their partner's skinny, some short, some fat and some bald. Honestly, who cares? There will always be people who find you attractive, and some who don't. The only person you ever need to worry about is yourself, and the love that you have for the way you are.

"You can be the ripest, juiciest peach in the world, and there's still going to be somebody who hates peaches." – *Dita Von Teese*

Mental health is just as important as physical health. So whilst the gym might be building your glutes and flattening your tummy, any pressure to stick to such a rigid routine is inevitably more damaging to your overall health than ditching the gym for a drive-thru cheeseburger ever would be. Let yourself live.

"Call a girl 'fat' once, and she'll never forget it." Tell me, in your lifetime, have you ever known 'fat' to mean something positive? I mean, there was a brief moment in R&B culture circa the early noughties when, if spelled with a 'ph', phat meant cool. Other than that? We generally use it to describe anything we deem substandard.

Almost the entirety of my childhood was spent constantly believing that I was too fat. It was a ritual for girls my age. A way of life. No one ever questioned it, we just proceeded with our lives feeling like we would never be good enough. When I was those four stones lighter, I spent my evenings on and off the scales counting every calorie and pound. I've been on some sort of diet since I was 13. A long while before I could even make decisions for myself and far prior to my body being developed enough to accept such drastic changes.

My very favourite read growing up were the Sweet Valley High books. I could get through at least one a night, and went to bed every evening dreaming of being a California girl with blonde hair, eyes the colour of the ocean and a tall, tanned and toned body. Yeah, my dream was to write for the school newspaper (we didn't have one), be a cheerleader (didn't have those, either) and date a kind and funny jock (definitely didn't have any of those). But instead I was chubby and unpopular and insisted on wearing various pairs of costume glasses to school. I didn't need glasses, I just thought I would be more fanciable as Dame Edna. Questioning of my downright strange fashion sense aside, I was desperate to be literally anyone else, and yearned to look completely different.

In a poll raised by the Health and Social Care Information Centre in 2015, 46.2% of 15-year-old girls thought of themselves as overweight. And, here in my twenties, it's difficult to think of any of my friends who haven't complained about their weight at some point.

Do you want your children and the future generations growing up believing they're inadequate? A difficult concept to come to terms with, admittedly. As a nation, we are often so focused on childhood obesity and the issues that are glaringly blatant rather than those that are perhaps more disguised. A healthy young woman believing she is too large, for example. It is, perhaps, this lack of attention that breeds such a high percentage of eating disorders in young girls. Why should fat equal ugly? I'm fat. In physicality, I am completely different to many of my friends and family. I feel no shame in using such a word to describe myself, because it's just that. A description and not a definition. My body type, weight or physical appearance doesn't determine who I am.

I'm not stupid. I understand the principle of health. I am well aware that being overweight can cause issues and complication with well-being. But, lest we forget, poor health is not necessarily synonymous with ugliness. Let's talk about said 'healthy lifestyle' people tend to harp on about, following the mention of the nation's favourite F word. I'm yet to see the anti-weight wankers attack smokers, drug users, alcoholics, workaholics and those indulging in unprotected sex about their lifestyle choices and the detrimental effect that it may or may not have on their long term health.

I am not promoting obesity. I am not promoting any one size. This is a message to urge you to find comfort and happiness with how you look; irrespective of whether that is tall, fat, skinny, short etc. There is no one 'happy' body type. You can be you, just as you are, and happy. Please do. Even if it were humanly possible to look at someone and immediately tell their medical history; shaming, humiliating and dehumanising them in any way will not improve their health. How can enforcing the idea on someone that they are insufficient and undeserving encourage someone to better care for themselves? Listen up, it is actually possible to exist in yourself and love your body without promoting anything. I don't see any of y'all jumping down Instagram model's throats because they are promoting big old boobs or the tiniest waist lines. I don't get shit from my hordes of haters when posting pictures of cocktails, claiming I'm promoting alcoholism? Doing something fun or feeling your outfit or the way that you look on that certain day, and then posting it on social media, isn't a promotion.

Nobody owes you a reason for the way they look. That is something that no human should ever have to excuse. How can this society preach so much about self-love and body confidence, and at the same time scrutinize and verbally bully such an enormous percentage of our population? I'll tell you why. People fat shame for the pure personal satisfaction of not being fat.

Your body is so much more than aesthetic. Your body houses you and is responsible for your abilities and keeping you alive by protecting your organs and innards. It's SO much more than what people see at first glance, and should be celebrated and thanked for that.

Your body changes. All. The. Fucking. Time. It's normal. It's natural. It's really hard to look back at pictures of yourself and not resent your current state, isn't it? I so often see and hear people complaining about wanting to get their body back. But, babes, it never left. Your body is the one you move and live in at present. It has taken you to where you are in this exact moment and for that, it deserves endless love, respect and thanks. Celebrate your ever-changing self. In this age of social media and selfies, it's hard as fuck to look back on old pictures and not hate on your present self. But you can. It's easy to look back in longing and through rose tinted glasses at your former self without remembering the shit storm that was raging behind the scenes. When I was my thinnest, I was constantly dieting. Constantly believing I wasn't good enough and constantly getting my sister to edit pictures of my body before I posted them online for public consumption. And if you look back and reckon that you were actually happier at that point in your life, then know that, rationally, that happiness was in no direct correlation to how thin you were. Now let that person and that picture go. You've outgrown them, for whatever reason. And that's completely normal. It's human. Allow yourself that, at least. Your body looks just right, right now. You will likely continue to grow and change further into the future. Trust your body, prioritise your mental wellbeing and give yourself a little more respect.

My self love and confidence is ever evolving. My body changes all the time, and ensuring that my self-confidence grows with it can often be a chore. Sometimes I eat 3 filled croissants for breakfast, and struggle to pull my skinny jeans up higher than my knees. Sometimes I gorge on a cheeseboard and then can't stomach anything else for the next two days. And sometimes my diet is vitamin and nutrient heavy, my skin is glowing and I feel radiant from the inside out.

The struggle is learning to love both, and all that's in between. It really isn't about always believing you look amazing, but understanding that, even when you're not at your best, change in your body is natural and should never be apologised for.

The fact that individuals are all so completely original is the pure definition of beauty, so give up on trying to alter anyone to your or society's ideals. If you have to diet to be a certain size, then that is not the size you are meant to be. There is no certain way you need to look. If you want a fucking cheeseburger then, bitch, I hope you get it supersize. Do whatever makes you happy because, at the end of the day, the approval you seek will only come from confidence within yourself. The confidence to be happy, live your life by your own rules and only do what you want. I want nothing more than for everyone alive to wake up and know how beautiful they are in that and every moment. Without make up or a six pack or a push up bra or a really great filter. And without cutting calories to get into a pair of size 10 jeans.

Chapter 40

Does chasing dick counts as cardio?
I've been doing it since birth.

I actively try and live a lifestyle as healthy as I can possibly make it. I try really hard not to eat bowlfuls of donuts for every meal, and I always have vegetables with my dinner. It counts if they're on pizza right?! I do what's best for my body; eating well and choking down that stubborn spinach that refuses to blend into my smoothie, but if I want a cake pop, then you'd be foolish to think I'd deny myself. Does chasing dick count as cardio? I've been doing it since birth. Other than that, I exercise only as and when I have to; despite perpetually telling myself that I really must get into yoga because I've heard it helps you live until 110, and I'd really like to do that. Unless riding my boyfriend counts as leg day, of course. Oh, and I'm fairly certain that fasted cardio and morning sex are the same thing. Being somewhat overweight and carrying a couple of extra kilos doesn't necessarily mean you're not healthy.

You know what really ticks me off? Whoever it was

that came up with body types, and how to dress for that certain shape. Bitch, don't you try and tell me what I can and can't wear, just because my arse is the size of a Jersey cow and my shoulders are broad. Listen, chicas. No one can tell you what you should wear. And fuck anyone that tries to (not literally, though – that might give them the wrong idea). Regardless of whether you're hourglass, pear shape, overcooked broccoli or broken slinky shaped – wear what makes you feel good and what makes you feel comfortable. And I don't care if that's tartan pyjama bottoms, glitter nipple tassels or a big old feather boa. Are you human shaped? Play up your natural sex appeal by wearing whatever the fuck you want.

"There is nothing more rare, nor more beautiful, than a woman being unapologetically herself; comfortable in her perfect imperfection. To me, that's the true essence of beauty." – Dr. Steve Maraboli

My biggest proclivity is anything remotely comfortable. These clothes aren't usually the prettiest or most flattering, either. I have been known to spend three quarters of a pay cheque on tracksuits, and have formed a sizeable obsession with pyjamas - they're all my Christmas lists consist of. But, in my defence, they are what I wear more than anything else. Don't trust anyone who chills in jeans.

The first thing I do when I get home on any given day

is tie my hair up and put my pyjamas on. Don't get me started on lingerie. When I was young and desperately seeking attention, I made sure to go everywhere in tiny little lace pants and a matching bra. And, for what? So I could end up severely uncomfortable sitting in the cinema, straining to pull my G-string out of my bum crack without causing a public scene? Don't get me wrong, I still have lingerie drawers boasting basques and babydolls, but more often than not I opt for the world's biggest pants. When I'm shopping for them, I actually search the web for 'massive knickers'. Hello, new realms of comfort. Of course, I have those that are comparable to old school bloomers for days and severe hangovers when comfort is the only option. I wear sexy underwear, rest assured. Mostly just to take Instagram selfies before changing back into my dressing down, but also if I'm in the mood to feel like a walking burlesque show. Which is most Saturday evenings, being totally honest. Plus, it's a lot more entertaining to get your tits out when they're encased in a cage of lace and straps.

I wear short dresses and cropped tops and leggings; and just about every other item of clothing that society tells me not to as a result of my size and body type. Fucking YOLO. I'll be damned if I'm on my death bed, wondering if my life would have panned out differently should I have ordered that tassel bralet and matching hot pants. This is my solemn vow that I will continue to wear, until I'm as old and wrinkly as I may be, whatever I wish, and whatever I feel the most comfortable in. So, yeah, if in about 65 years there's an OAP wandering down your local high street with her enormous cotton briefs hanging out the back of her sequined mini dress, then you'll know it's me.

Television shows like *The Biggest Loser* and glossy magazines showing bikini-clad celebrities boasting cellulite and a couple of kilos that might not have been present a month prior promote the ideal that 'fat' is bad. Remember the social uproar when Protein World unveiled their latest body-shaming ad featuring a very toned, slim, young woman in swimwear and the caption "Are YOU bikini body ready"? Because the world would likely stop should we all don a bikini, step on the beach and announce ourselves 'bikini body ready' right there and then, without enduring their hideous protein shakes and meal replacement bars. The only thing you should have to do to become 'bikini body ready' (it's so gross to even type) is put on a goddamn bikini. That is all. Your worth is not measured by the size of your waist. I wanna see fat girls getting the guy in movies. I want to see runways brimming with 'big girls'. I want someone to attend the Met Gala and really blow people's minds, just by being fat.

Want to know how I got my bikini body this year? Pizza. And wine. Lots of it. I ate and drank what I wanted (within reason) and did what made me happy. And then I dug out an old favourite Speedo swimsuit (you'll soon learn that the only things I'm really prepared to spend money on are prosecco and obscenely low cut dresses) and put it on. And proceeded to strut around Europe with my body exposed in all its wobbly, lumpy, jiggly glory.

As a community and population, it's well overdue that we take a step back, a long, hard look in the mirror and give up on scrutinizing literally ANYONE else to make ourselves feel better. Self love means accepting yourself and loving the skin that you're in - regardless if that's a size 6 or 26. Your feminism isn't feminism if it isn't completely intersectional. By telling other beings that they have to change their bodies or stop eating white carbs (bitch, please), you are not empowering anyone. Not even yourself. By shaming someone for being overweight – no matter how 'helpful' you are trying to be in looking out for their health – you are tearing them down.

As an example, why is it that we don't consider tall women as attractive as tall men? It seems as though tall men are always favoured over their shorter friends. And, I get it, having a man twice the size of you can make you feel little and dainty - I swear I only started dating rugby players because their thighs made mine look smaller. So what is it about the same situation vice versa? Unless their height is teamed with a stick thin body, the cruel 'big girl' subcontext is so hard to shake off. Do men stereotypically find smaller women attractive as a credit to their masculinity? Quite possibly, but I'm willing to bet that those men wouldn't turn down a roll in the hay with a 5'10 supermodel.

My sister is tiny. I'm talking size 6, watermelon boobs, Pamela Anderson on steroids type physique. And so naturally, she attracts a considerable amount of attention. This doesn't bother me – I've always had my own plethora of wannabe suitors. But what bothers me is comparison. I don't believe in doing so, but apparently, other people do. And I've actually been told that I'm not as skinny or as hot as my sister. I'm hot in completely different ways. We are completely different people, with a completely different look and I am completely inclined to punch you in the neck if you think it's ever OK to compare us.

I have a beautiful family. I'm not at all impartial, but I can confidently say that anyone reading this would fancy at least one of my cousins – they are all gorgeous. And, again, I'm not just saying this because we share the same genes. Genes we may share – but jeans we definitely cannot. The majority of my cousins, namely ones of a similar age to me, have all been blessed with the same genetic structure as my sister. And I mean they're all naturally very slim. And subsequently, I have always been the 'fat cousin'. They were dainty and pretty as little girls and I was chunky and a tom boy, and always had to play the prince or the knight or swing around the garden in my knickers pretending to be George of the Jungle. I wasn't the princess or fairy or literally anything even remotely feminine or girly. Honestly, I wasn't bothered at the time. I was pretty rough and tumble (most likely as a result of my antics as George), and I could brush it off. But as I got older and started to understand that I looked a little bit different to everyone else, it started to bother me more and more.

It's tough growing up and looking different. It's even tougher when you're older, and seemingly everyone else on Instagram also fits a certain mould. But it is so important to embrace your differences. The little things that set us apart from everyone else is what makes our beauty individual. All of those things that make you cringe when you look in the mirror; your spots, stretch marks, cellulite, scars, rolls, freckles, body hair etc, are all part of your amazing being. And, again, we should be completely and utterly grateful for our bodies and the amazing things that they can do. Why are we pushed to constantly scrutinize ourselves when our bodies are strong and able. They carry us, allow us to do amazing things and keep us alive. We should be praising them daily but, instead, find ourselves stood in front of the mirror every morning picking out faults.

I make a daily effort to enforce an affirmation. I wake up, stare straight in the mirror and identify assets that I like about myself that day. Sometimes it's an ode to my thick thighs and chunky legs. I thank them for allowing me to walk and taking me where I need to go every day. Sometimes it's my stomach, which I blissfully regard for not only letting me eat, but for bravely standing out in glorious rolls – allowing women and other people that follow me to see that I look just like them. Often it's my boobs, and I look forward to one day hopefully getting the chance to let them fulfil their natural purpose and giving life and strength to another being. And, occasionally, it's something minor, like being thankful that my nail and toenail polish matches. Or that I'm having a great hair day. Regardless of what it is; no matter how significant or substandard you may deem it – daily affirmations are important and impactful and something we should all encourage.

Now, you've all read my ode to body positivity, and you know that I am comfortable and happy in the divine shell that is my body. But know that self-love doesn't come from nowhere. Almost all advocates for bopo, self confidence and, actually, almost everyone I know full stop have experienced some form of body shaming. Whether it conscious or not. Your response to the amount of space that my body inhabits, defines you and not me.

It is crazy that in this society we live in, women are shamed for how much sex we have and how much food we eat. Like, how DARE we enjoy our miserable lives filled with pleasures, eating delicious food and having orgasms? Monstrous. I plan on leading a long and happy life drinking prosecco like it's going to fall off the face of the earth, ordering a side of fries over salad, buying new clothes rather than dieting to fit into those I already own, and growing out all of my hair like it's nobody's business.

Chapter 41

Not shaving my barely-hairy legs at fourteen didn't make me any less smart, forgetting to wax when I first bedded the guy I'd had a crush on for a year didn't change my wicked sense of humour, and refusing to waste any more of my 'adult' life doubled over in the bath and ridding my lady garden of any and all shrubbery won't make me any less beautiful or sexually appealing.

I like body hair. Seriously, I've never been one to shy away from an up-close and personal encounter with a pube. I love hairy men. Men with hair on their head, chest, arms, legs, back, sack and crack. Equally, I'm rather fond of female bodily hair. Sorry, not sorry if I have such a life which results in me forgetting to shave my armpits for 6 weeks – I live in Britain, and I need it for warmth.

I have actually undergone laser hair removal on all sections of my vagina most often seen by the public (bikini line, mostly). My reasoning behind said hair removal? It would be nice to see my bikini bottoms every once in a while. Besides the pain of the laser, it was nice to be horizontal for 20 minutes (or 45, if you're growing a national rainforest like me), listen to the calming music and rise some time later, smooth and carefree (direct translation to rashy and uncomfortable, but nonetheless...).

Back when I was 14, and had convinced myself that losing my virginity was on the cards, I was obsessed with spending my Friday evenings, hunched over the bath with my legs akimbo - in most unflattering positions - attempting to rid my vagina of every last pubic hair. For over a decade of tiresome years I've been hacking at my bodily hair, ambitiously wishing to awake every day with a body as bald as a coot. But simultaneously whinging about how I couldn't wait until I was 'grown up' so I could embrace my au natural self. And, sure, as this continued for the next few years, it became force of habit. I pretty much mastered the ever tricky 'reach around' - necessary for an entirely silky smooth nether region. For a day or two post shave it was glorious and I would swan around my bedroom in tiny lace knickers, taking naughty pictures of and obsessively stroking my brand new bald lady garden.

This fixation would be short lived, however, when I woke the next morning to find my perfectly smooth downstairs was now host to an array of angry red lumps and bumps; razor burn was my very worst enemy. No matter how sharp the blade, how expensive the razor, or how much I exfoliated after shaving, two days post preen I'd find myself in worlds of discomfort. Queue me then spending my Sundays spread eagled on my bunk bed, furiously lathering myself in layers of Aloe Vera. By the time I'd cured myself/learned to live with my breakout, regrowth would be all up in my grill and it was time to trade the lace thongs for cotton granny panties. All that for a handful of hot nudes…

From then I ruled it best to leave shaving strictly for special occasions. I.e. when I thought I might get lucky. Before a night out, I'd bathe for hours, scrubbing, shaving, exfoliating, moisturising and plucking every inch of my naïve body just in case a handsome man showed me some attention in one of my favoured Friday hangouts. I was obsessed with being hairless and perfect, because 'boys don't like hairy women', don't you know. And, naturally, they'd only want to see me again if my fanny was smooth to the touch. I became somewhat obsessed with having the perfect vagina. I would become enraged having spent such hours landscaping, to end up wasting a shave. I mean, how dare men not want to have sex with me after I skipped school to tango with Gillette's finest?! It would throw off my grow-back schedule and leave me open to the dreaded risk of stubble. That I certainly do not miss.

It didn't take me and my feisty, feminist demeanour long to figure out that shaving for anyone other than yourself was completely pointless. Your body should remain in your control, and you should never let anyone tell you what to do with it. If your personal preference is fully hair free, then veet away. If you like a landing strip, make sure your razor doesn't slip. And, if shrubbery is more your kind of thing, lie back and let it grow. Do as you damn well please, and should you be unfortunate enough to encounter someone who criticizes or turns their nose up at your choice, a swift kick to the shin should send them flying out the bed and, with any luck, the door. A close shave, if you'll pardon the pun.

Personal preening is important, but equally as important is to do so in whatever way you're most comfortable. I used to dream of my future life as a 'proper grown up' (married, with a stable job and a bank balance that allows for the purchasing of unnecessary breakfast cereals twice a month) and fantazise about the day that, at long last, I could stop fussing about with my pubes. I so looked forward to going native. And just like that, one day I realised that it was time. By no means was I married and I certainly (still) can't afford fancy cereal, but I lost sight of the point of doing literally anything that I didn't want to do for myself.

Post laser, my bikini line grows back at pleasantly low speeds. For the most part, I leave it be, often revelling in delight at the smooth and baby-like hair that graces my vagina's presence. The only bodily hair I ever really feel compelled to get rid of is that under my arms, and only as result of fear of luring in wild animals who fancy me as one of their own. I am naturally a very hairy person (even more so now my ovaries have formed an alliance against me). The thick dark hair I have on my head and am so often complimented on means just as thick, just as dark hair almost everywhere else.

Yeah, porn stars have vaginas not dissimilar to pre-pubescent teens and yeah, lots of men and women prefer to keep their pubic area similarly trimmed, but let me assure you - shaving your fanny until it resembles a Lidl chicken breast will never tickle everyone's fancy, so why waste your precious time doing so if it's not what you want? Admittedly, my boyfriend prefers it when I don't look like I'm smuggling a small family of otters in my knickers but, with the exception of being in a bikini and in the more-public-than-usual eye, I much prefer to let it all hang out and go back to basics. If not for myself, then for my lovers. I think it only polite to remind them that they are in fact performing cunnilingus on a woman, and not a girl.

How has it become so offensive to have pubic hair in our generation and society? Not twenty years ago, a woman's bush was something to be worshipped and fawned over, similarly to how the newer, balder version is now. Why has this changed so suddenly and severely? Growing up, I was often privy to my naked female family members (we're a very open family), and, in short, was raised by the bush. So imagine my sheer horror at being teased and strictly informed at high school that pubic hair was disgusting and just not the thing to be seen with. It is drilled into young women and girls that having hair down there is not alright – when, in truth, it's nothing short of normal. I would put my last tenner on this taboo being the direct result of underage boys watching porn and making their minds up that women are meant to be smooth, hairless creatures with pale pink arseholes and a passion for the taste of cum.

Please, if you're reading this, think of your mothers, grandmothers and all the women who paved the way before you, proudly boasting a bush. It's not gross, it's not unhygienic and it's not a repellent for creatures who want to bed you. Trust me, I am writing from years of experience. And life is seriously too short to not have the fanny hair you want. Seriously. Body hair is not the enemy and it pains me to see girls as young as ten and eleven (and I'm sure even younger) endlessly plucking their eyebrows and shaving their limbs in an extreme effort to conform to the standards of their peers. Whilst still at Scottish school (bear in mind I was only there until I was fourteen), I was mocked and teased by the girls in PE who had seemingly perfect, hairless, fake tanned pins and lived to laugh at my slightly chubby, pale and hairy calves. And I didn't cave. In all fairness, this was mostly down to the fact that my mother (empowering me from the youngest age) refused to let me touch my body with a razor until I was almost sixteen and going to my first pool party.

There is just no point conforming. My bush is the new black. Be individual, it's a lot more fun. If you wanna wear navy and black together and mix prints and patterns, then you go for it! Wear your hair in crazy little buns all over your head - very alien chic. Who cares?

I don't think people actually read Vogue, I personally think they just pay a fiver to look at the pretty pictures. Fashion is what you make of it. Everyone else is already taken, so you may as well be yourself. Not shaving my barely-hairy legs at fourteen didn't make me any less smart, forgetting to wax when I first bedded the guy I'd had a crush on for a year didn't change my wicked sense of humour, and refusing to waste any more of my 'adult' life doubled over in the bath and ridding my lady garden of any and all shrubbery won't make me any less beautiful or sexually appealing.

I am, in no way, saying that undergoing mane-tenance makes you any less of a woman - simply just that, for me and my preferences; pubes are the way forward. So consider this my official resignation from the razor. I am sooooo done with paying nearly £50 a month for someone to scald my labia and leave me sticky and unable to walk properly for hours. From now on, I am embracing my inner cave woman. Criticize and judge me all you want - I am so relieved to finally draw a line under preening my pubes. And don't pretend you won't be jealous when I'm at the pub an hour before you simply because I no longer have to spend an extra fifteen minutes in the bath, bent over like a contortionist to try and get a clean shave on my bottom. Sorry, not sorry.

As previously mentioned, the day I could quit shaving and waxing forever was one I looked forward to for a very long time. If I didn't before, dating some rugby chap back in 2014 changed my opinion on everything.

He was really mean to me, and I loved it. I wanted to chase him and make him fall in love with me so people could dub me as some wild rugby hunter and tamer. Obviously, this didn't go my way and I ended up the victim of a(nother) hump and dump. Tragic. Anyway, on one of the few dates that he did take me on (and before I'd given him my precious flower), he explained to me the strong and passionate hatred he had… for pubes. He showed me a picture of a woman he'd dated previously - who, may I add, was some incredibly gorgeous, Mediterranean-looking babe in her early twenties. It wasn't until he told me that he pulled out of their first sexual encounter mid foreplay, and called things off that I recoiled in horror. It was beyond me how such an arrogant and sexist man had won the affection of such a woman in the first place, but to turn her down because she hadn't waxed?! Mind. Blown. Unfortunately, I can't say that it put me off him and I didn't let him enter my perfectly shaved nether regions the following week, because it didn't. But it is something that has been etched into my brain ever since.

"If you retain nothing else, always remember the most important rule of beauty, which is: who cares?" – *Tina Fey*

I hope it's now well etched into your memories that I don't believe in having regrets. I don't regret sleeping with that complete knob of a man (I've repeated that mistake more times than I'd care to admit) and I don't regret ever shaving any part of my body. I just wish I could go back to my younger self, wishing the years away so she could finally grow her pubes out, and ask her 'Why Not'?

WOMAN UP

Chapter 42

Use every occasion as an excuse to celebrate your vagina.

Use every occasion as an excuse to celebrate your vagina. She can give you children and, more importantly, orgasms, and this is the kind of versatility that we all should be living for. Your little lady really is a miracle, and deserves to be treated as such. I've heard Kourtney Kardashian swears by slathering hers in yogurt. Whilst dairy products are not my fanny go-to, I take special care and effort in making sure she is washed every day, and fed and watered as often as possible. I know it's hard because marketed products often have flavours like 'Unicorn' and 'Butterfly Wee', but you literally only need water to clean your vag. Anything else and you run considerable risk of contracting an infection. Vaginas are meant to smell. Obviously, if the smell is putrid, then please see your doctor or OBGYN, but from what I've read on my favourite vagina doctor's Instagram, you can smell a healthy vagina from a metre away.

It's not natural for them to smell like candied

strawberries, and nothing grinds my gears quite like feminine hygiene products specifically manufactured for your front bottom. When have you ever seen a section of the pharmacist brimming with products promising cleaner, nicer smelling penises? You can contemplate for as long as you like, but the market does not exist. Because, naturally, male genitalia is sooo much cleaner than that of a female. The vagina is self-cleaning. It is so smart, that it actually cleans itself - that's magic right there. No dick can do that. So how has it become expected for women to douche and spritz our vulvas with products boasting names and subtle hints such as 'fresh', 'intimate' and 'your fanny shouldn't smell like a fanny it should smell like a fucking hydrangea bush'. It's just so not cool.

It goes without saying that if shower gel isn't good for your happy valley's PH, neither is anything foreign. And do you know what the worst thing you can insert into your vagina is? Food, and especially those with high sugars. Granted, what you put into your body via your mouth will have an effect on your nether regions, but I'm referring to what you're putting into those regions directly. I mean ice cream, sweets, chocolate and especially those God awful glitter pouches you can insert up there to ensure your lover is well and truly vajazzled by the time you're finished. A gal pal once dealt with Britain's three-and-a-half days of summer by having her boyfriend stick ice lollies into her muff. Don't be fooled into fantasizing about a mini milk, or even an ice pole; she opted for those big, fat, 9inch rainbow fuckers. And, whilst in the moment it was super sexy and refreshing, in the long run; it was sticky, tricky and resulted in chronic Bacterial Vaginosis.

Please, please, don't use food to masturbate with. Learn from both my friend (with the kipper-scented vagina she had for a week) and me, Lady Nell of Carrotville. Use regularly cleaned sex toys, your hands or real life human beings. And you'd be right to have doubts about the real thing matching up to your perfect plastic pal. Because, let's be honest, it is completely and entirely different. But if the size of the steed isn't floating your boat, at least try a different position or a different partner. Size only really matters when opting for either a 'medium' or 'large' McDonald's meal.

WOMAN UP

Chapter 43

Much like we women are expected to have a shaven bush and a mouthful of semen at all times, porn teaches boys and men that, in order to properly service a sexual partner, they need to be packing some serious length and girth.

This begs the question that women everywhere have been asking for centuries... Is a huge beef baton really what we want? A ten inch dick would be longer than my forearm, I measured it this morning. I believe the average willy-wielder is around 5 inches. The longest officially recorded is 14 inches, whose owner suffers dizziness when he gets a hard-on. And, even though he's heterosexual, can only have anal sex as his member can't actually fit into a vagina.

Discriminating against penis size is not body positive. We've got to celebrate all shapes and sizes, and this doesn't just refer to hourglass figures with minuscule waistlines and boobs bigger than your average. It means acceptance for all; big girls, small boobs, curves in all the non-stereotypical places, literally any shape or size under the sun. And this also applies to men and anyone identifying as anything else. Body positivity is so female oriented and it's become fashionable to have bigger girls catwalking (about bloody time), but there is so little press and attention on male body positivity. So this is for the bigger guys, the skinny guys, the short guys, the guys with stretchmarks, the guys with small dicks, the guys with man boobs, the balding guys and the super hairy guys. All of you. You are recognised, appreciated and should be celebrated.

Instead of fannying around with your online dating bio, claiming you'll only date guys over a certain height, why not just not say anything, instead? Make yourself a cup of tea and remember what your mother always told you; if you don't have anything nice to say, then keep your gob shut. It's body shaming, and that just doesn't sit well with me. You'd absolutely lose your shit if you came across a guy's profile professing that he only wants a girl under a certain weight.

So we all know by now that I'm a big old hoe and spent the majority of my teenage years underneath strangers. Ah, memories. As I'm sure it's not difficult to imagine, I've had my fair share of almost every kind of human sausage possible. I hope it brings you some joy to learn that the men I've been with who have been well-endowed have never topped my 'best shag' list or, indeed, beaten their smaller opposition because of size alone. In all honesty, most of them were too big, and ended up being painful and quite frankly annoying. The average vagina is only 3-4 inches deep. 3-4 inches! And, whilst some may have a depth of up to 6-7 inches, the national average just isn't meant to play host to battering ram-like third leg.

Of course, a lady's Sarlaac Pit is designed to accommodate the odd large object. For example, the tiny human that may or may not lever its way out. But this is not during intercourse and absolutely does not make it at all comfortable or fun to have huge objects jammed with force into your hermetically-sealed shame basket, bumping repeatedly against your cervix. Fucking ouch.

So, contrary to popular belief, bigger is not necessarily better. I'm just going to go ahead and add that to the long old list of stigmas that we're breaking down. I mean, for me it's hard to imagine meeting and not instantly fancying someone vertically gifted. Back to tall men. There's something about them that makes them stereotypically attractive. Emphasis on the 'stereotypically', here. Again with the dating profiles; this is more than likely the reason behind so many men lying about their height in theirs. Perhaps it's that, when seen as tall and therefore big and strong, they tend to make anyone of not similar inches feel that much smaller, and like they could protect you and/or lift you up and slam you into a wall whilst entering you. It's absolutely vital to keep tall friends for use as a human shield in an alien attack or zombie apocalypse, too.

I think we're kidding ourselves if we claim that part, if not most, of our attraction towards those who tower above us is because we'd expect them to be hung like a horse. But, my penis-possessing friends, I can assure you that no height is more attractive than another. My first string of semi-serious relationships were all with partners under 5'8. Guilty as charged; I've done my fair share of stereotyping, this variation included. As a result, I have often met tall men and instantly bedded them, wishfully expecting to be greeted by enormous girth. I've fallen disappointed by this high hope before, but, sometimes they are just as you'd imagine.

I would say large and in charge, but I don't necessarily mean that they were in control or indeed even knew what they were doing. I'm an emotionally unstable person as is, so envisage how distressed I get when snake charming a man with a substantial sausage, only to find out he just doesn't know what to do with it. All the gear, but no idea. It happens, and, whilst I know the line between pleasure and pain is often thin, to be in such a situation is unpleasant AF. Hence making it my mission to stop cherry-picking budding bonks based on their height and how large my friends had heard their dicks were. And, honestly, I started having really great sex. Sex with people that I connected with and gave a chance to make me laugh pre-sliding in.

It is, in turn, all about how you use that weird looking one eyed trouser snake. I've had sex with a couple of people verging on forearm size, who obviously (and obnoxiously) assume that because of the size of their (not so) little General, they don't need to put in as much work. Well, let me correct you. It feels like you're being repeatedly stabbed by a large tree branch completely at random. No rhythm. Just prodding. And no woman has any chance of climaxing whilst constantly worrying about which of her innards you're about to rupture.

On the flipside (literally), your booty hole can be between 5-7 inches deep. One of BOB's fairly flexible relatives could just about push past that, but only to take the gateway to hell into the large intestine - providing you're really patient, flexible, have a bucket load of lube at your disposal and way too much time on your hands. And, of course, you don't mind things being inserted into your actual internal organs. A rock-hard love stick, on the other hand? Hmmm, not so bendy. 10+ inches might sound like a good time but like a right-wing government, for most people at least, its better in theory than it is in practice - and think about it, the longer the dick? The closer to the ovaries. It's like shooting a gun in close range. Pump, pump and BANG you're pregnant. Please don't quote me on that, though. It might come as a surprise for you to learn that I'm not officially medically trained.

If you're shooting for realistic sex and you're not overly keen on ring sting, you may want to reconsider parting those thighs for anything of frightening size. As hard as it is to believe; no, I'm not a poet, either.

Much like we women are expected to have a shaven haven and a mouthful of semen at all times, porn teaches boys and men that, in order to properly service a sexual partner, they need to be packing some serious pubic inches. It's just not true. I love porn, but you'd be a fool to take it at face value. So, while a massive shlong may be a welcome treat once in a while, those all too rare fellows who really put in the effort, regardless of size and girth, are at the top of my 'to do' list all day, every day. My range of previous partner-given orgasms has stemmed from those with smaller-than-a-snicker to full blown super soakers, and everything in between. Alas, it is no easy feat to make me climax. Make no mistake, I am a pro at doing it myself and, with years of practise under my belt, have whittled my time down to under a minute. Those who have shot and scored are not necessarily of the same ilk; i.e. all enormously endowed, but have been few and far between.

Imagine if women could only get pregnant if they came during sex. There would literally be like six people on every continent. All too many men think it is acceptable behaviour to work until they get theirs, but not until you get yours. I don't waste my time putting in all the effort to get you off, for you to finish and forget about me. I want equal rights everywhere; economically, socially, and definitely in the bedroom.

Chapter 44

Vajaculation.

Tell me, what springs to mind when you hear the words 'female ejaculation'? For me, it's the brutally clear mental image of a platinum blonde porn star, with double F tits, squatting over a hugely hung man and furiously rubbing herself until she leaks her love juice all over her mate's chest. I'll be damned if the majority of you even know what female ejaculation - or vajaculation - is. It's something that I, personally, have sat and pondered about on many an uneventful evening. Ain't no Friday night like one spent googling the inner workings of the vagina whilst ploughing through a family sized M&S microwaveable lasagna. I remember being 16 or 17, and being asked if I could squirt by one of the putrid pubescent teen boys who I was texting at the time. I knew I couldn't (or hadn't) but that didn't stop me from spending hours of my summer holiday locked in the bathroom drinking pints and pints of water and trying to 'completely relax' as I came multiple times. Still, nada. Reportedly (thanks Google), there are two types of ejaculate that come from a woman. You either release a small amount of white-ish fluid on climax or alternatively, a much larger amount of liquid, leaving a mark not dissimilar to that if you'd wet the bed. If you haven't yet already, then perhaps you have resigned yourself to the fact that you're not a squirting Sally at all. While it's believed that we don't all have the ability, I have a sneaking suspicion that this rumour was probably generated by a group of men who couldn't quite get their girlfriends there.

Whilst we're on the subject of wetting the bed, though, it's time to put the rumours at rest. Both types of female ejaculate, as described above, originate predominantly from the equivalent of the female prostate, before being expelled through the vagina. But don't be too worried about taking a leak on your partner, it's likely that it happens subconsciously anyway. Not quite golden showers, but considering the close proximity of the urethra and the vaginal opening, it's probable that you're sharing pee particles more often than you'd think. Regardless, it's a beautiful thing and should be illustrious as something historic and glorious. The Aphrodite's fountain of the lady garden.

After the long and tiresome years spent searching through the hundreds of thousands of suitors (if only) for he who could make me squirt (I'm a firm believer in 'there's no such thing as can't' and there's probably a man out there for every woman just waiting to make her sort of pee herself), I finally struck gold. Ah, my first ever internal orgasm that came from someone other than my plastic pals. Before meeting my current boyf and his award-winning willy, this was the most beautiful member I'd ever laid my eyes (and almost every orifice…) on. And, considering the male genital region has a tendency to look like a naked mole rat, this really was extraordinary. The most notable asset was the shaft curvature which made it possible for him to reduce me to a quivering, heavy breathing mess in a matter of seconds. At present, it's hard to call whether or not the orgasm was as 10/10, as I remember it, or if I was distracted by the soothing tones of his Floridian accent as he whispered sweet nothings in my ear and continued to call me 'lil lady'. Without offending an entire nation, he had the kind of voice and accent that made me want to don a cowboy hat and elope to the Deep South.

Now, for those of you who haven't yet found someone to make you replicate the feelings and facial expressions of doing something uber embarrassing in public, don't be afraid to get out there and find them. Whilst I remain to be in full support of appropriately used dating apps and appropriately worded bios, I would be willing to bet my most favourite throw pillow that men who claim to be able to make you squirt in their personal bio will likely do so before cutting your limbs off with a hack saw and burying you under their patio.

Your other option is to invest in one of the fabulous g-spot vibrators that the multitude of toy shops pride themselves in. Slightly more expensive, but guaranteed to be noticeably less hassle. The only way I can describe the feeling of vajaculation is as a slightly sloshy, very intense explosion of pure filthy yet angelic pleasure. Like a *Scissor Sisters* music video. The first time, it took me a good six minutes post-cum to recover.

Whilst our love affair was pretty much over before it began, I do have the Southern gentleman to thank for opening my eyes to a world of pleasure I had not yet experienced. Having my first solely internal orgasm and début ejaculation ushered me into a world where sexual selfishness was not an option. Now I know it's reachable, I always go for gold. For so long I offered myself up as a living, breathing sex doll – someone that could be shagged but would leave having surrendered to little to no pleasure. It's no way to live your life and, if you find yourself relating to the above, feel free to fuck off and find yourself a partner willing to put in the time and effort to transport you to cloud nine.

Allegedly, some men can be repulsed by the thought of ladies getting their freak fountain on. Hilarious, really, considering how repulsed most women are by so many of the typical behavioural traits embodied by men. And yet here we are. Most men that I've met, however, find it incredibly arousing to be able to perfectly pleasure a woman in such a way - and there's almost never any chat about urination. I've also read that lesbian couples are more likely to make each other squirt than a heterosexual couple as a result of the mutual respect and comfort around each other. I'm suddenly flooded with what ifs…

Also, maybe it's just that bit easier to find the G-Spot with a finger, as opposed to bashing around at it with a meat log. Just something to consider.

Way back when in 4th Century China, liquids excreted during orgasm were believed to be permeated with mystical and healing properties – and, in current day, people are questioning the existence of the marvel that is the G Spot?! It kills me to have to explain, but it is one to two inches into the vagina on the front wall, and bears an almost bumpy texture. Ribbed, for your pleasure. If anyone ever asks, I am forever grateful for Gloria Steinem, bagels, spanx and what are by far the strongest muscle in my body; the kegels which I have been working on since I was about 15. I originally started exercising them after reading a baby birthing book and being terrified that one day my vagina might too meet with my bottom to form one large and very painful tear. No babies or vaginal stitches yet, I hasten to add, just excellent sex from yours truly and her often very tight vagina.

Jesting aside, I recommend working out your Kegels or as you might know them, pelvic floor muscles. And this comes from someone who hates physical exercise with a passion. But something you can do whilst in your PJs watching Saturday morning TV? Sign me up. Try squeezing as if you're holding in a wee for as long as you can, then letting go and repeating. I also often do them at my desk and repeat as many times as possible, you know, before I have to go into a meeting or something. And although it often looks like I'm straining for something, pulsing them mid-bonk drives him mad. And it can make him finish quicker. You know, if he's over-running into the second half of Bake Off. It's probably important to mention that it's not all that great to practice when you actually need the loo – holding in a wee can have detrimental effects on your lady system and could even leave you incontinent.

Chapter 45

You've got to be clitting me.

A climax via G spot is statistically the hardest to obtain. But, if all else fails, opt for the love button. Fun fact, the clitoris is actually enormous. Only the tip is visible, but the full length stretches around the vaginal tunnel and extends out towards the thighs. And contrary to popular belief; vaginal orgasms are also clitoral. The G-spot is actually just an internal section of the clitoris. There are so many unknown facts floating around about that gorgeous little man in a boat – and, for Christ's sake, why? We should be praying to the O Gods every evening and hosting dedicated TED talks. It's a beautiful thing but, not only is it seldom talked about, it's also one of the most endangered species on earth. I'm joking, but I still struggle to understand the difficulty in locating it amongst most male lovers.

"In 1969, we put a man on the moon. In 1982, we invented the internet. In 1998, we discovered the full anatomy of the clitoris." – *Jesscia Valenti*

And yet, here we are, in the twenty first century, only dreaming of pleasure whilst our one-night mate furiously rubs our pubic bone. You've got to be clitting me. Honey, just no.

Whilst we might not typically brag about it, women actually get a 'boner' 20-40 minutes into sexual arousal. When our body feels like 'yeah, ok, I'm ready for the shagging now', the pea in your pod stiffens and grows larger, a similar action to that of a penis. Unlike the multi-purpose penis, the love button is designed solely for sexual stimulation. Not dissimilar to a pork sword, a clitoris can completely differ in size, depending on the person. However, this does not directly correlate with the level of pleasure that the mini-yet-almighty button can supply. Actually, it has been claimed that the clit extends up to six inches inside the female body – meaning it's basically bigger than the average penis.

What's more, there's a ton of research suggesting the penis and clitoris start out as the same thing before different hormones cause each to develop in their own gender-specific ways. And who tried to argue that big dick energy could only be radiated by a man? Yeah, sit yourself down.

Back in the 1970's, women were totally obsessed over their clit. It was a beautiful time for all. The love button became an empowerment symbol for many of the second-wave feminist movement, who were regularly heard singing the chorus "We don't need men, we have our clitorises". If I had a voice that sounded less like a wailing new-born Basset Hound, I would consider re-releasing it as a single. According to the Museum of Sex, the outer (visual) part of your clit contains around 8,000 sensory nerve endings. Making it not only the most sensitive part of a woman's body, but also a shit load more sensitive than the penis, which only contains half as many nerves. I know I've rattled on about female ejaculation and the importance of discovering your G-Spot, but medical reports show that 75% of all women are unable to orgasm during intercourse without some form of clitoral stimulation. Understandable, really.

Pleasure-seeking is a natural part of the human make up. With a companion or alone, virgin or not so - women everywhere are seeking the big O. Back in 2012 it was calculated that, on average, approximately 285,193 people of the five billion sexually active people at that time were having an orgasm. Every second. And that was six years ago – imagine in comparison how many people right this second are saying yoo-hoo to their woo-hoo.

Some might even go as far as invasive surgery on their hunt for pleasure. Stand back, designer vagina. There's a new 'down there' surgical procedure in town. It is said that ladies are now undergoing the knife to alter their clitorises. This particular procedure is called "clitoral unhooding", and is thought to heighten sensitivity. On the other hand, improving sexuality through surgery will always carry a risk of scarring and infections; inevitably meaning no sex life at all. Similarly with clitoral piercings. I've always admired the 'gem on your gem' idea, and I think they actually look quite sweet. From friend's reports, the tiny piercing totally improves all aspects of sex, but there are more than a few horror stories floating around as told by women who've lost not some but ALL feeling in their bean. *Shudder*

When considering any surgical procedure (not just those with the potential to ruin your sex life), think long and hard before signing yourself up. Make sure you've exercised every possible option in clitoral stimulation before you rule yourself 'de-sensitised'. There's more often than not an option you haven't explored, which could open your eyes to simultaneous stimulation and pleasure. So do it. Familiarise yourself with Clive the clit. There's no shame in having a little fumble in your knickers when daytime TV just isn't cutting it. You're forgiven for fancying masturbation over *Cash In The Attic*. Use alternative body parts, household objects and a variety of toys. Practise with a variety of different pressures, techniques and, like me, partners. Ensuring you're completely relaxed will also give you a leg up (or leg over), and if practising with your mate, don't be afraid to tell them what works and what doesn't. If anything, they'll thank you for your guidance.

The orgasm has limitless benefits, including pain and stress relief and prevention of incontinence. So don't be alarmed when I call you out on your 'techniques'. You're not digging to Asia, love.

Chapter 46

*Maybe I'm not oversensitive;
maybe you're just a dickhead?*

I get a whole lot of criticism on my hyper-sensitivity. I am one for taking the piss out of myself literally all the time, so it's not that. It's my reaction to people making jokes about things that are just not funny. Like Madeleine McCann, fat people and Jimmy Saville. You just don't know who you're going to offend.

"Maybe I'm not oversensitive; maybe you're just a dickhead?" – *Sophie King*

And it's the same with making rape jokes. After this book is eventually published, a whole lot more of you will learn of my ordeal, but it isn't something I broadcast often. And so, people make jokes about it in front of me. I can't bear to hear, let alone say the R word, and hearing people use it in such a jovial sense fills me with deep and despairing sadness.

Despite knowing better, I often browse the

comments section on Feminist Facebook posts. It's disgusting. People are horrible. And then they complain that everyone is oh so sensitive 'these days' and it's ruining humour?! How about we just don't make jokes that, in effect, are normalizing what the joke is about. So rape, child abuse, sexual harassment, misogyny. The more jokes are made, the more people laugh at them and the more the line between what's OK and what's not is blurred. I'm actually really funny (don't pretend you haven't giggled at least once so far), I love a good joke and my best days are those spent laughing until my stomach aches. And I appreciate humour, in fact, it's an asset I value higher than most others - I just don't sit well with mockery. I can see why people use humour as a coping mechanism. But your coping mechanism shouldn't have the potential to hurt someone else; that's just not fair.

The unpopular opinions trend that has recently taken the internet by storm happens to apply to almost everything but real life issues. How about: unpopular opinion – we should stop making real life situations into a punchline. I'm actually all for the #UnpopularOpinion trend. It is giving people a voice and a platform to share their honest thoughts without scrutiny. I mean, other than the keyboard warriors who have a lot to say about almost everything. But we can chose to ignore those for now and forever, right? Because YES to new and unheard voices. That is the beauty of opinion; everyone is allowed one and, again, providing you don't utilise this to behave like a prat, it's pretty awesome that the internet and Millennials in particular have created this safe space to share. I love it and, other than those about politics and left-wing-isms that I wholeheartedly agree with, my favourite to date are the hailing of pineapple on pizza, that money can, actually, buy happiness and that an Aperol Spritz is a shite cocktail and tastes like bad perfume.

There are certain words and phrases that it's high time we cut out of our vocabulary forever. Obviously, words like depressed, psycho and crazy as mentioned previously, but the list is substantially longer than most of you would care to consider. How about using words like 'retarded'? Why would you ever think that was OK? Mocking people and using critical terms to describe someone or something in a negative light brings an entire curtain of pessimism over that particular word. It is not your word to abuse.

I feel the same about the word 'classy'. People describing themselves as classy makes me shudder from the inside out. We cannot separate people by class, it's not the fucking 1930s. I just can't deal with this bullshit hierarchy; having more money and a fancier house or more designer shoes than someone else does not make you a better person. You know what the worst part of the movie *Titanic* is, for me? It's not when Jack tragically dies because selfish Rose couldn't make room for him on that enormous door. And it's not when her evil fiancé physically assaults her. It's when the ship is sinking, and they lock the gates to the lower decks, meaning no-one could escape. Instead of having the hassle of trying to save them, they chose to let people of a lower class die as a result of their social status. I have to switch off at this point, because the sheer fact that this could ever be allowed to happen makes me simultaneously livid and devastated.

I don't like the word classy. What's more, people have taken to using this word as an opponent to the insult 'slut'. As in, you can only be ridiculed for having sex, but you'll be praised if you opt out of intercourse and wear sensible-length skirts. Reality TV shows flaunt beautiful girls claiming to be classy, and 'not that kind of girl'. Excuse me if I'm being obtuse, but what exactly is that kind of girl? Someone who takes full control and enjoys a healthy and thriving sex life? She doesn't sound so bad. And so why can we not be both classy AND that kind of girl? What is it about our sex lives that demeans our status? On the subject, how can we deem someone not worthy of the C word by the way that they dress? We've all heard people say that they're opting for a classy outfit because, apparently, class can't be granted if you've got your tits and/or legs out. Pffftt. What a load of shite.

Let's be honest, classy isn't just anointing someone to belong to a higher class; it's congratulating them for not being associated with the impoverished masses. It's almost 2020. We're working on equality. There's no time to segregate individuals based on their income, race and fashion sense. The word classy makes me feel dirty. And not because I feel like I don't conform, but because demeaning people based on their social class is old-fashioned and discriminatory. Don't be a snobby wanker, basically.

In direct correlation with the classist adjective, comes 'ladylike'. Nothing grinds my gears quite like someone telling me my behaviour isn't ladylike. Um, hello, I've got a vagina and I identify as a woman. How much more like a lady can I be? I swear a lot. And I mean a lot. I come from a family of cursers, but even they don't eff and blind quite like me. I find it an almost artistic form of expression and use it regularly when other words just won't do the job – and that's OK! Angry, sad, happy, excited, sooooo over Monday mornings? Swear. Insults? Much better accompanied by a rude adjective. I am so often told to stop swearing, that it's unpleasant and unladylike and unattractive. To which I only ever have one response - Fuck off.

Being 'ladylike' essentially means being stereotypically respectable, polite and charming. Never having a cross word to say about anyone or anything and always being approachable. Bitch, please. I refuse to conform to anything that tells me what I can and can't do with my facial expressions. If I want to frown, and fully embrace my resting bitch face; then I'll be damned if I do any different. And don't tell me to smile. OK, we good?

Women do not owe you time, conversation or

politeness. On the whole, we are only told to smile to appear more aesthetically pleasing. If we get technical - asking a woman to smile, essentially pressuring her into doing something she is not comfortable doing, is harassment. If I look like I don't want to be approached, then chances are, I don't. I tend to smile when I'm enjoying myself. If it doesn't happen around you, that's just not my problem.

It's not my personal preference, but that doesn't mean I haven't been made aware of the attacks on women who have decided that having a baby isn't in their remit. It's getting boring me constantly yelling at you all to do what you want, isn't it? Well goddamn stop letting other people influence your decisions, and start making your own mind up about your own life! I find this conversation hard to bear. True, it's no doubt that we were initially created with all the lady parts for one reason; to reproduce, but who says that we still have to live in a by-gone era? Sorry, 1950s, my husband makes his own dinner. Back to the point – it isn't a necessity for every living female to mother children anymore. Independence is incredible, and should be something cherished. Not everyone is meant to have babies. Your life will be just as love-filled and enriched as everyone else's – but just with something that you are more interested in and passionate about. And that's bloody admirable. I plan to have lots of cherub-like babies, but that doesn't mean you have to. Women are complete human beings, not potential mothers. Motherhood is an option.

"We have been made to believe that a baby is basically a magical agent of change and that having one will, in one fell swoop, make your husband love you more, make your life more meaningful and, above all else, is the best thing you will ever do as a woman. I didn't care about any of it." – Radhika Vaz, Unladylike: A Memoir

So, are we done with telling people that there is only one possible way to behave like a lady? Let's call it quits. Being deadly serious, I was told the other day (by a male colleague) that women shouldn't use the toilet for anything other than a number one because THAT wasn't ladylike. Please note – this isn't specific to just work loos. Let's crush that common analogy that "women don't poo". Because, news flash, we do. Just as much as everyone else. And, while I'm here, we don't have a precious pink rosebud in place of our arsehole, either. Ladies? Feel free to do your goddamn business anywhere you please (but do try and keep it within a bathroom, I'd hate for you to take my advice too literally and end up squatting in the street *Bridesmaids* style).

Obviously, real ladies don't sleep around either. Yep, the Queen of the Hoes is back to tell you to do more shagging, again. I spent my single years totally throwing my cat around – and I loved every minute. To almost every single or newly single guy or gal pal I stumble across, I offer the most helpful advice that I can, which is just fucking shag whoever you want. Providing you aren't hurting anyone (yourself included) physically or mentally, go out and do it. Or don't! It makes no damn difference. You already know of my passion for sleeping around.

And, whilst we ladies are fucking on the first date, let's take a vow to eat and drink what we want, too. My girlfriends used to avoid dinner dates like the plague so as not to have to eat in front of their suitor. Admittedly, I've developed into quite the opposite and have no issue inhaling half a double cheeseburger in four minutes on a date (complete with fries and various other side dishes, obvs).

I'm gunna be pissed if I need to give another lecture here on diet culture and why it's often actually healthier to be fat and happy. Mental and physical health? Both important. Insecurities and constantly thinking you should look/be a certain way? Psychologically damaging. Aaaaand, exhale.

You'll need something to wash all of that delicious grub down with, too. And getting drunk is yet another behaviour frowned upon by the ladylike elders. Have we met?! No, seriously, I'm actually asking because often I'm SO drunk that have to I re-introduce myself to people because I just can't remember meeting them for the first, second or even third time. I, for one, like the way I feel after 7 glasses of prosecco, and I find it utterly hilarious to get absolutely wankered and laugh about the most stupid things with my favourite people. And I will be forever entertained by how much like Beyoncé I think I am after a few sherberts and a spin on the dance floor. So, no. I will not apologise for drinking so much that I leave a shoe in the club bathroom, forget where I am and my left boob pops out every 3 - 5 seconds.

Listen, honey. The term 'ladylike' is bullshit and seriously gets on my tits. If you identify as a woman, then you're a lady. Having immaculate manners, standard female genitals and a chastity belt does not earn you the right to call yourself a 'lady'. It's refreshing to embrace being a living, breathing human being; and not the cardboard cut-out they expect us to be. Wear the short skirt, kiss the handsome stranger, eat the goddamn burger. You do you, and make sure not to give a tiny rat's ass about anyone else along the way. Let's smash the stigma surrounding what it is to be and act like a woman.

Chapter 47

The last chapter.

This is the last chapter of my book. THE LAST CHAPTER! I am currently doing that hysterical, panicky half cry, half laugh and reaching for my vibrator or glass of cheap Pinot; whichever my fumbling hand finds first. I can't believe I've actually written this thing. I started years ago, and my memory stick with the initial 11,000 words and notebook with every story and shag I could think of were stolen during a family trip to Rome. It took a fair few years to get back into it, but here I am. And, without sounding like I'm accepting an Oscar, I want to thank my mum, dad and the academy, for taking a chance on an unknown kid.

I'm totally joking, but I really do owe a tonne of thanks and a good few bottles of this surprisingly good and not completely vinegar-like Pinot to my family and friends – that super support system I was rabbiting on about. If I can write a book about 25 years of life and sex, you can literally do anything.

I am grateful for my life panning out the way it has.

Without the various mishaps and experiences, I wouldn't have been able to fill the pages of the masterpiece that you're reading now. I don't believe in having regrets.

As much as it pains me that I'm attracted to them, I really do love men. I know a lot of these pages could be conceived as me being totally anti-bloke, but I'm just not. I owe a huge amount to men. My dad and family members, exes and even one night stands; they have all taught me such huge lessons that, without them, I never would have learned. In fact, men are probably to thank for my feminist transformation. I can almost guarantee that without the penis presence, I would still be in a girl-hating ruck, letting men use and abuse me to their heart and dick's content and saving sex for the third date. Oh, and I'd undoubtedly be spending my life counting and tracking everything I put in my mouth (both wiener and calories included) and opting for slimline tonic. Yuck.

I didn't write a book to boast about sexual conquests (although you'd be forgiven for assuming), and nor did I do so to beg for sympathy. I didn't jot down my trials and tribulations to get one over or get back at anyone. I wrote these words in hope that someone will read it and relate. This is my story, my life so far and the journey and lessons I have learned. It's about my take on feminism and being able to process what has happened to me to encourage the belief that you can do so too. I am a normal girl in her mid-twenties. I have been through some shit, and I have come out the other side. I am hungover, battered and bruised, have stretch marks, scars, cellulite, body hair and a big old fat arse.

I have a serious penchant for prosecco and anything carb-based, and could spend hours talking about my passions. I also have enormous dreams. Seriously; dreams bigger than my ego and arse combined. I desire nothing more than to witness the coming of true equality in my life time. I want a successful career as an activist and humanitarian, an enormous litter of babies and a nice new handbag. But, for now, you're most likely to find me in a beer garden, champagne flute in one hand and menthol cigarette in the other, frantically trying to apply red lipstick with the few fingers that aren't preoccupied.

"*I write for those women who do not speak, for those who do not have a voice because they were so terrified, because we are taught to respect fear more than ourselves. We've been taught that silence would save us, but it won't.*" - Audre Lorde

Life is what you make it. I'm trying not to get in too deep here, and so am tip-toeing around the Dalai Lama type speech that I could reel off at any time. So, whilst you're busying yourself removing all traces of toxicity from it, don't take anything in life too seriously. Apart from toxic people. Remove them, and then be happy and carefree. Oh, and Chlamydia, because it's treacherous when left.

Have your own opinions. If they are racist,

discriminative or in any way cunty, then keep them to yourselves or as far away from me as possible. Otherwise, I love hearing about everyone's different perceptions of the world. Don't be afraid of making them known; the best thing about opinions is that they are never wrong, because they are completely personal. There is so much joy in going to the pub to tell people that cottage cheese is the devil's work, children between the ages of four and 16 are annoying and double denim is a trend to be cherished. I like to do these things and then walk away. Dramatic like a mic drop, but considerably less cool.

Just fucking laugh it off. Embarrassing things happen to everyone, like, all of the time. I'm sure my youngest brother thought it would be hilarious to pull my bikini bottoms down on the beach, exposing my bearded clam to most of Southern Portugal. Whilst at the time, I thought it appropriate to drown him, I can now laugh about it. And pray that I never see anyone from Portugal again.

I was a very sad person for a very long time, so I know the advantages of laughing your ass off. As well as having a shit tonne of health benefits!

Do you think this glow came from a bottle?! No no, this is from many hungover Sundays spent with my boyfriend, family or fabulous peers, laughing until we can no longer breathe.